A Dog Who's Always Welcome

A Dog Who's Always Welcome

Assistance and Therapy Dog Trainers Teach You
How to Socialize and Train Your Companion Dog

Lorie Long

Wiley Publishing, Inc.

Howell Book House
Published by Wiley Publishing, Inc., Hoboken, New Jersey

Library of Congress Cataloging-in-Publication Data is available from the publisher.

ISBN: 978-0-470-14248-6

10 9 8 7 6 5 4 3 2

All photos by Ralph and Lorie Long
Book design by Lissa Auciello-Brogan
Cover design by Wendy Mount
Book production by Wiley Publishing, Inc. Composition Services

To the dogs of my past:
You continue to walk by my side in spirit.

To the dogs of my present:
You bring a unique joy to every day.

To the dogs of my future:
You are my as yet undiscovered treasures.
I can't wait to meet you.

And, to my husband, Ralph, who "gets it" about
me and dogs.

Contents

Chapter 5

Chapter 6

Chapter 7

Chapter 8

Acknowledgments

For encouragement, insights, and answers to my endless questions, I extend my deepest thanks to Brian Jennings, Sheila O'Brien, Lydia Wade-Driver, Danielle Moore, Marilyn Wilson, Elizabeth Broyles, Connie Knisely, Cabell Youell, Ann Hogg, Nancy Patriarco, Jan Stice, Jeanie Calhoun, Kali Kosch, Karen Hough, Linda Eaton, Maggie Blutreich, Elsa Larson, and the St. Francis puppy raisers. Dogs have no better friends than all of you.

For providing me with a map of how to bring a passion for ideas about dog training to print, I thank my agent, Kate Epstein.

For the gentle guidance and occasional tough love it took to make this book the best it could be, I thank my editor, Beth Adelman. You knew where we were going right from the start and you showed me the way. Thanks, Beth.

For enduring the travails of being married to a writer with a deadline, and for sticking it out to see how it all ended, I thank my husband, Ralph, a great doggie dad.

It takes two years and costs between $7,000 and $20,000 to acquire, raise, and train a highly skilled assistance dog. Many disabled recipients receive their canine partner free of charge. The training centers rely on charitable contributions to support their efforts. Please consider contributing to the following assistance dog training centers when you plan your charitable giving. You will give the gift of independence to a disabled person and the gift of honorable work to a good dog.

Thanks from all of us!

St. Francis of Assisi Service Dog Center
P.O. Box 19538
Roanoke, VA 24019
(540) 342-DOGS
www.stfrancisdogs.org

Blue Ridge Assistance Dogs, Inc.
P.O. Box 229
Manassas, VA 20108
(703) 369-5878
www.blueridgeassistancedogs.info

Assistance Dogs of America, Inc.
8806 State Route 64
Swanton, OH 43558
(419) 825-3622
www.adai.org

A Dog Who's Always Welcome

Introduction

The George Mason University campus is nestled on a grassy, tree-shaded wedge of land in Fairfax, Virginia, an upscale suburb of Washington, D.C. Surrounded by traffic-clogged streets, overbuilt bedroom communities, and a population of professionals, corporate executives, diplomats, and government employees, the school caters to a population of highly diverse commuter students.

During the late 1990s, I regularly sped from my nearby corporate office to this campus to attend evening courses. And, on most of those occasions, I encountered another student and her assistance dog, a beautiful Golden Retriever, on their way to her classes. Although she and I never attended the same classes, I watched them both on campus, through several semesters, with great interest. She and her dog fascinated me.

I had been training my own dogs and teaching canine obedience classes to the public, privately, and as a volunteer for a local dog training club, for more than twenty years. I had taught beginner through advanced students the skills and techniques they needed to mold and modify their dogs' behaviors in a way that created an obedient family dog. I had even taught students how to train their dogs to compete in American Kennel Club obedience trials. Hundreds of dogs and owners had come through my classes and achieved various levels of success.

I instructed my beginner students about how to teach the commonly used "good manners" commands to their dogs, such as "sit" and "down" and "stay" and "heel." At that time, most trainers still relied on the choke collar, strong verbal commands, an occasional treat, and repeated training drills to teach behaviors. The other club trainers and I spent a great deal of time teaching students how to work with their dogs, using these tools in a humane way.

Generally, though, I wanted the dog and owner teams graduating from my obedience classes to achieve a higher level of partnership. But I wasn't entirely sure what was missing from my training program. Some students did a fine job of using the training techniques, and their dogs reliably displayed the asked-for behaviors. However, other students could barely contain their dogs in class. These dogs rarely stopped lunging at other dogs or people in the class, constantly pulled on their leashes, whined or barked, dug in the dirt (we taught classes in a horse barn), barreled in and out of the car, and tripped their owners because they were always underfoot and in motion. Once in awhile, by the end of the session, these hard-to-handle dogs would sit or heel when signaled to do so; their owners complained that the dogs would obey their signals perfectly at home but would not honor their wishes or take direction in public.

Soon, positive reinforcement training techniques replaced the militaristic methods of choke collar corrections and punishment. Thankfully, these aversive styles of training were no longer the preferred methods of modifying dog behaviors. They were replaced by food rewards, play training, shaping desired dog behaviors in a positive way, and allowing undesirable behaviors to extinguish themselves by not rewarding them. The dogs in my classes learned behaviors faster and were happier using these positive training methods, and the owners felt better about the training process.

All the instructors advised their students to "proof" the training of dog behaviors. We told the students first to teach their dogs a behavior at home, such as "down." Then, to proof the dog's ability to perform the behavior in public, we suggested that the students take their dogs to the park, or to a friend's yard, or to the parking lot of the library, and practice the "down" command. Including proofing in my training program did produce some improvement in a dog's ability to perform away from her home training environment, but most students found it to be a long, tiresome, and frustrating process. Later, when I started learning from service dog trainers, they helped me understand what was missing from this approach.

Did the dogs in my classes become better overall companions or family members as a result of the change to more positive training methods and proofing? To some extent, yes. But I still heard complaints about how the dogs did not perform reliably in everyday life. What was still missing?

At the university, I watched the disabled student's assistance dog exhibit an entirely different type of companion dog behavior. The student was confined to a wheelchair. Her dog reliably demonstrated behaviors such as picking up dropped items, giving money to the cashier in the student union coffee shop, walking next to the wheelchair without lunging no matter the speed of travel, pushing doors open, and lying down quietly when his owner paused. The dog acted with complete decorum while cars whistled past her in the parking lot, when a student dropped an armful of books only a few feet away, and when someone at a full run shouted from one end of a noisy corridor to the other right behind him. The dog commuted by car, walked through automatic doors, took the elevator, stood in many lines with his owner, and waited quietly while she ate her snack in the cafeteria.

This is the kind of dog every owner really wants, I thought. Sure, he's capable of responding to signals like the dogs in my obedience classes. But he can do so reliably in a public setting. Not only can the dog obey commands like "pick up my dropped keys," but he can work in public without any loss of performance. Even more important, this dog can conduct himself in an acceptable way in a highly variable environment, even when he's not responding to a specific command. He demonstrates self-control and the ability to focus on his owner in the face of strong distractions and unfamiliar conditions. He is a take-anywhere companion dog—the dog most people have in mind when they make the commitment to add a dog to their family.

The disabled owner, of course, was not physically capable of teaching or refining her dog's behaviors using a choke collar and a leash. She was in a wheelchair. She couldn't physically manipulate the dog into any particular position or hold him there. She couldn't stop him from running off or catch him if he did. Her work with her dog relied on her voice, and, probably, the use of treats. So she had even fewer training tools than the able-bodied students in my obedience classes.

My students didn't need a dog who could open doors or pick up dropped keys. But they really wanted a dog who would behave properly in public—a dog they could take to the beach house rather than leave in a kennel, a dog who could remain in the living room when Aunt Lily came to visit instead of spending the evening barricaded in the bedroom, a dog Mom could safely walk on a leash without dislocating her shoulder, a dog who could travel in the car without chewing the upholstery, a dog who didn't lay back her ears and try to bolt when asked to enter an elevator. The "good manners" signals were useful, but of limited value if the overall demeanor of the dog prevented her from joining her family outside the home where the signals were most needed to help the dog understand how she should behave.

I wanted to find the key element of dog training that could produce that kind of companion dog. So I decided to ask the trainers who teach dogs like the assistance dog I watched at the university. Obviously, they knew something about how to teach a dog specific behaviors, *and* they knew how to teach a dog to successfully handle the rigors of everyday life in the company of her human companion. They knew how to produce a dog who could do a job because of her training, and who was always welcome in the company of humans because of her social skills.

I suspected that these little-known assistance dog trainers had a secret that most dog trainers and owners did not know. I thought they might have the answer about what was missing from most family dog obedience training programs. And they did.

Chapter 1

The Quiet Experts

Imagine you are the mother of a 5-year-old boy with Down syndrome, a genetic abnormality that causes mild to moderate delays in physical and intellectual development. Although capable of functioning successfully in many ways, your son, Robbie, has difficulty maintaining his balance while walking. You want him to be as independent as possible, but he doesn't have the physical skills to navigate on his own. Even after receiving physical therapy, Robbie still needs help.

You've read about guide dogs who help blind people and about assistance dogs who open doors and pick up dropped objects for their owners. You decide to try to find a pet dog who might be able to somehow help your son.

In the Sunday newspaper, you notice a classified ad placed by a breeder for a litter of Standard Poodles. You remember that Poodles shed very little and don't produce much dander, thereby making them an excellent choice for owners who suffer from allergies or asthma, or who just hate to vacuum the house all the time. You know that Standard Poodles are large dogs, which means they will have the physical size and strength to interact with a child with mobility issues, who may tumble over or suddenly grab onto them for support. You also know that Standard Poodles are lean and graceful for their size, not broad and massive like Rottweilers, which, in your thinking, would make Poodles easier to manage physically. You decide to buy one of these pups for Robbie.

After a few months, your dog has matured into a lovely, pure white, adolescent Standard Poodle named Jane. She and Robbie get along wonderfully, and you've had no trouble housetraining Jane or teaching her a few simple signals, like "stay" and "down." But Jane cannot be as effective a companion for

Robbie as you had hoped because she wants to play much of the time and her preoccupation with games interferes with her ability to help Robbie. When visitors arrive, Jane becomes excited and difficult to manage. Easily distracted in public, Jane cannot stay calm while you are walking in the park or spending the afternoon at the playground. She dances around trying to interact with other dogs and people, wants to chase squirrels and rabbits, and pays little attention to Robbie. When he leans on Jane for balance and support, she sometimes loses focus, speeds up her pace, and Robbie falls down. Now it's harder to manage Jane and Robbie together than it was to manage Robbie alone. Jane is not the helpful, take-anywhere companion you had envisioned for Robbie, although she has brightened his life considerably at home and he loves her dearly.

Thankfully, you do not surrender Jane to the local animal shelter in exasperation, and you refuse to just leave her home all the time and abandon your hopes of finding a helping companion for Robbie. You do a little research and find an assistance dog trainer who provides the missing element necessary for shaping Jane into a polite, focused, take-anywhere companion dog: managed socialization training.

Two keys unlock the full potential of a dog to become a fit and enjoyable companion for his human owner. One key is behavior skills training, in which you teach your dog the particular behaviors that will make him an acceptable companion, such as responding to your signal to wait for you to tell him to go out the door, rather than having him barge through the doorway and knock you over on the way out. Behavior skills training addresses the physical skills you want your dog to have as your companion.

The other key is social skills training, in which you teach your dog the social skills necessary to function as an acceptable inhabitant of the complex, contemporary environment in which he lives, such as remaining calm and quiet in an elevator or a motel room. Social skills training addresses the emotional skills you want your dog to have as your companion.

Assistance dog trainers are unique among the ranks of dog trainers in that they have refined a highly successful and very efficient method of securing the second, and most elusive, key to creating the perfect companion dog—social skills training.

Assistance dog trainers work for assistance dog training centers and foundations across the country. Some provide assistance dog services through their own private training firms. These trainers rarely teach the standard dog obedience classes offered through local dog training clubs, county recreation departments, pet supply shops, and the like. They don't become television personalities or publish quirky training books. They quietly and regularly produce a succession of dogs with the behavioral and social skills required of a true companion animal.

Assistance dog trainers do have a lot in common with dog obedience class instructors: They are skilled in teaching dogs specific behaviors. However, assistance dog trainers add a critical ingredient missing from many standard obedience training curriculums: a systematic, well-defined, carefully managed dog socialization plan.

Let's take a look at how assistance dog trainers raise and train the dogs. We can start by understanding what the dogs must do and where they must do it. Once we understand the trainers' goals, we can tap into their training secrets and discover how they can help you and your dog.

DEFINING THE TERMS

What is socialization? It's the process of desensitizing any living being to a wide variety of environmental conditions and situations through repeated exposure. Some trainers call it "habituation," "desensitizing," "exposure training," "life skills training," "behavior modulation training," or even "environmental inoculation." Socialization includes training a dog to manage himself in diverse environments.

What is managed dog socialization? It is a well-planned approach to the socialization process that efficiently develops positive outcomes and desired results. We might also call it a positive-outcome socialization program.

Proper socialization is a crucial element in the upbringing of assistance and therapy dogs, and it's also vitally important in the upbringing of all dogs, including family dogs whose owners envision their pets as companions they can take almost anywhere, who will live comfortably and politely in the home, and who will conduct themselves with good manners in public.

Assistance Dogs

Founded in 1987, *Assistance Dogs International (ADI)* is a coalition of not-for-profit organizations that train and place assistance dogs. ADI hosts seminars and meetings for assistance dog trainers. Its mission statement also includes the following goals:

- Educating the public about assistance dogs
- Ensuring the legal rights of people with assistance dogs
- Setting the standards and establishing the guidelines and ethics for training assistance dogs
- Improving the bond of the dog-partner team

According to ADI, "assistance dog" is a generic term for guide, hearing, or service dogs specifically trained to do more than one task to mitigate an individual's disability. Dogs used for protection or personal defense are not included in this definition. Classified under the umbrella term "assistance dog" are:

- Guide dog: a dog who guides blind or visually impaired individuals. Guide dog owners rely on their dogs to safely negotiate the unseen environment.

- Hearing dog: a dog who alerts deaf or hard-of-hearing individuals to specific sounds. Hearing dog owners rely on their dogs to indicate the presence of unheard but important sounds in the environment.

- Service dog: a dog who works for individuals with disabilities other than blindness or deafness. Service dog owners rely on their dogs to perform physical tasks or to provide assistance in a medical emergency.

- Psychiatric service dog: a dog who supports individuals who have a condition attributed to a brain chemistry malfunction or to emotional distress. Psychiatric service dog owners rely on their dogs to help them cope with panic disorder, depression, post-traumatic stress syndrome, agoraphobia, and other such conditions.

Each of these types of assistance dogs lives in the home with their disabled owner and is trained with the goal of mitigating their owner's specific disabling conditions.

Most assistance dog trainers refer to the owner as the "partner," indicating the close and mutually respectful relationship that develops between an assistance dog and his owner.

Many people think assistance dogs help only severely impaired partners, such as blind people or people in the last stages of a degenerative disease such as multiple sclerosis. However, many assistance dogs support mildly disabled partners who just want to live independently without becoming a burden on family members, who want to maintain employment, who want to avoid pain, or who may need help in a crisis. Performing simple tasks such as bringing a phone to the partner, opening a cupboard with an attached strap, or tapping a floor pedal to turn on a lamp can sometimes make the difference between a comfortable life and a life of frustrating dependence for a mildly disabled person.

Assistance dog training takes place in several stages:

- Early puppy training: If the assistance dog organization has bred the prospective assistance dog for its program or a breeder plans to donate a puppy to the group, early behavioral and social training begins in the first weeks of the puppy's life. Dogs who enter an assistance dog training program from a shelter or from a home environment will not have this portion of the training program, but still can work successfully.

- Training with a puppy raiser: When a puppy is ready to leave the litter, assistance dog training centers place the puppy with a *puppy raiser*, an individual or family selected by the center to socialize the puppy, begin to teach him a few basic obedience skills, and prepare the puppy to enter the formal assistance dog training program. Puppy raisers attend classes with the puppy to learn and practice, under supervision, behavioral and socialization techniques. They maintain the puppy in their care for six months to one year.

- Assistance skills training: Staff trainers teach the adolescent dog the specific behaviors needed to mitigate the disabilities experienced by his prospective partner. When the puppy raiser returns the dog to the center at about 1 year old, the staff trainers begin this more formal training, which lasts about four to six months.

- Working assistance dog follow-up training: Usually conducted monthly for the first year following placement with a partner, and annually thereafter, follow-up training ensures that the partner understands and uses the proper methods to teach the dog new behaviors, and continues to provide socialization opportunities for the dog.

Assistance dog trainers manage all stages of training and monitor the progress of each dog, making recommendations about changes to the program to suit each individual dog and partner.

For the family dog owner, the later stages of assistance dog training that teach specific helping behaviors are interesting but not vital. But the socialization and basic obedience training, the training that produces the foundation on which all the rest of the dog's training and ultimate success rests, is of critical importance to any companion dog.

Public Access

Assistance dog partners and trainers enjoy the benefit of public access guaranteed to them by the Americans with Disabilities Act (ADA) of 1990, a federal civil-rights law. This legislation gives a person with a disability the right to be accompanied by their assistance dog in all places that are open to the public. It also gives assistance dog trainers the right to work with a dog in public places so they can replicate real-life situations in the training program.

To comply with the terms of this legislation, an assistance dog must be well-behaved and under the control of the partner or trainer. By definition, the ADA therefore recognizes the importance of proper socialization for dogs. It acknowledges that dogs who will be expected to function with decorum in the human environment must be able to experience full exposure to that environment and practice the skills needed to function there. The ADA addresses the importance of trainers preparing dogs to accompany people in need, not only by teaching the dogs the behaviors required to assist their partners, but also by teaching the dogs how to conduct themselves in public. Assistance dogs in training and in service wear jackets or vests to identify them when they're out in public; trainers and partners refer to this as "being dressed."

As the owner of a family or companion dog, you do not have the same public-access rights. Therefore, you and your dog will not have the same rights as a disabled person and their dog to enter a supermarket, a retail store, or a restaurant. But you will not need your dog to accompany you to all of these types of places, as disabled partners do.

You can expose your pup, or maybe your young dog, to all the situations where you will need your dog to behave as an adult. If you own a dog with whom you plan to compete in agility, for instance, you want a dog who can stay with you in a motel room, as my dogs do when I travel to an agility trial away from home. If you rent a house at the beach every summer, you want a dog who will not damage items in an unfamiliar environment and who can walk on the beach without bothering other people or dogs. If your brother's family comes to visit and they want to bring along their well-behaved family dog, you want a dog who will not be aggressive to polite canine visitors.

There are plenty of opportunities to expose your dog to environments that will be a part of his life—*if* he can conduct himself in a socially acceptable manner.

Therapy Dogs

Federal law does not define the term "therapy dogs." Usually, they are personal pets who work with their owners to provide friendship and the therapeutic benefits of contact with animals to a wide variety of people. They are not limited to working with people with disabilities, but may also help hospital patients, retirement-village or nursing-home residents, prisoners, and even provide assistance with remedial reading programs in public schools.

Unlike assistance dogs, therapy dogs do not have specific goals that define their work with people. They are not asked to improve their partner's physical mobility by picking up dropped objects or to be able to dial 911 on a special telephone in an emergency. Therapy dogs offer the simple emotional benefits of contact with animals by visiting with those who appreciate animals but do not have access to them. The visits are most often arranged by the recreational therapist or activity director in an institution, rather than by the medical or rehabilitation staff, and much of the visit content may be spontaneous.

The Delta Society, an international not-for-profit organization of pet owners, volunteers, therapists, educators, veterinarians, and others, provides training and support to therapy dog handlers. Founded in 1977, it registers therapy dog teams who have been screened and are prepared to conduct pet therapy work. In its *Team Training Course Manual*, Delta identifies some of the benefits that can accrue from therapy dog visits:

- Entertainment and amusement: There's nothing like a few silly dog tricks to get lonely or sick people chuckling.
- Mental stimulation: People may recall fond memories of their own pets.
- Human socialization: People laugh and interact with one another in the presence of friendly, happy dogs.
- Pleasant touch: Petting a friendly dog is a safe, non-threatening, and non-painful touching interaction.
- Outward focus: Patients are encouraged to focus on the dogs rather than on themselves.

Therapy dogs can be purebreds or mixed breeds, and come in all sizes and types. Their owners may have acquired them from a breeder, from a shelter, or even as a stray. They all have a few things in common: They love to be in the company of people, and they have been socialized by their owners to act appropriately in the therapy environment; and their owners have the unselfish desire to help other people by sharing the companionship of their own dogs with those who also love dogs but do not have one.

Therapy dogs must function in a challenging environment. In a nursing home, for instance, the floors are slippery, the air smells of medicine and disinfectant, and there may be scraps of food or even a dropped pill on the floor. It might be hotter than the dog is used to. Usually, several therapy dog teams visit together as a group. Each dog must accept the presence of the other dogs and handlers, and might have to tolerate close contact such as riding the elevator with another team or two. Elderly residents with declining motor skills might pet them a bit awkwardly. People might go by in wheelchairs or with walkers. In the midst of all of this activity, the dogs might be asked to walk around wearing a Halloween costume and politely "shake hands" with each of these strangers. And, of course, the handlers can't jerk their dogs around for mis-behaving, raise their voices, or chase their runaway dogs around the facility.

Therapy dogs might know only a few signals for a few simple tricks, but they must know how to conduct themselves properly in this highly complex human environment. They have not been bred specifically for a therapy dog program, they have not been trained by a professional assistance dog trainer, and they have not been required to learn any complex behaviors, other than what their owners think might be amusing or helpful. They are everyday dogs and members of everyday families who have been socialized by everyday own-ers who have included a managed, positive-outcome socialization program in their dog's basic training. Many therapy dogs do not begin their work until later in their lives. But due to the good socialization they received in preparation for therapy work, they can take on this new activity and flourish.

ROBBIE AND JANE

About a year ago, Robbie's mom met with Karen Hough, a private assistance dog trainer in southwest Virginia. Karen has short, strawberry blond hair and piercing blue eyes, and she impresses me most with her soft-spoken, collected demeanor when working with dogs. Karen is a veteran dog trainer who has worked on the staff of a service dog foundation and has taught dog obedience classes in the area. Recently, she launched her own professional dog training business, Field of Dreams Dog Training.

Robbie's mother hired Karen to teach them how to refine Jane's behavioral training, add new behaviors to her list of skills, and socialize her so that she can accompany Robbie in public as an asset rather than as a liability. Occasionally, Jane stays with Karen for a few days for more intensive training. Karen refers to Jane's developing canine social skills as the dog's "life skills."

On a cool day in early spring, I accompanied Karen and Jane (who was wearing a balance harness that Robbie uses to steady himself) to a strip mall where she had taken Jane for training the day before. "Yesterday, Jane did a fine job in Best Buy and in Staples," says Karen. "But, she lost it in PetSmart, where I was requiring her to behave herself and give me a couple of specific behaviors despite the presence of other, unfamiliar dogs in the store. I could tell she was a bit stressed, so we're here today to work through the problem."

Karen described Jane's training as "late stage training," which means train-ing a dog who has already learned good social skills but still needs to polish those skills a bit further. She described how well Jane had proceeded through the social skills training, which allows her to accompany Robbie almost every-where he goes. Actually, after watching Karen and Jane in PetSmart, I thought

Jane was by far the most polite and controlled dog in the shop. Most people would think of her as a highly socialized dog. But Karen had read the subtle signs of stress and lack of focus in Jane the day before, and knew she needed to help Jane work through these issues to improve her performance. "Losing it" to Karen did not mean Jane was lunging at other dogs in the store, barking incessantly, or pulling hard on the leash. It meant that in that environment, Jane was not quite able to provide a couple of behaviors when Karen asked for them. Karen never raised her voice above a soft, conversational level in the store, nor did she jerk Jane's collar or manhandle the dog in any way during the training session.

"Probably, I will be keeping an eye on this boy and his dog for the dog's whole life," says Karen. "His mother will want me to watch for slips in training or social skills that need supporting. Any owner can do it, but in Robbie's case, the results are so positive I think I'll be working with them into the future."

How assistance and therapy dog trainers socialize dogs so thoroughly, customize the training for each specific dog, recognize the need for further training, and turn out highly companionable animals, one after another, from all types of backgrounds, is the story of this book.

Happily, the story of Jane and Robbie and Robbie's mom has been transformed from a melodrama into a tale about the value of canine service. It's also a story about the mutual joy of companionship experienced between a boy and his dog.

You and your dog can live that same kind of story.

Chapter 2

Hallmarks of a Dog Who's Always Welcome

Let's paint a mental picture of a well-socialized companion dog—a dog who's always welcome. We can ask the assistance dog trainers to help get us started with a general description. Whether the assistance dog trainer is working with a future hearing dog or service dog or guide dog, preparing that dog to function properly in everyday life as the companion of a human is the vision that underpins the entire training program. That vision frames all the work assistance dog trainers do in their various activities with the dogs. And the vision holds true for the family companion dog, as well.

Of course, assistance dogs, their trainers, and their partners work together as teams. This suggests that assistance dogs don't become well-socialized or trained by osmosis or by chance. The inclusion of a planned, positive-outcome socialization program managed by the dog's handler remains critical. Therefore, our mental picture of the well-socialized assistance or companion dog should include an image of the dog's trainer, as well.

First, we'll turn to ADI for a general picture of an assistance dog working in public.

ADI'S MINIMUM STANDARDS FOR
ASSISTANCE DOGS IN PUBLIC

1. Public Appropriateness

> Dog is clean, well-groomed, and does not have an offensive odor.

> Dog does not urinate or defecate in inappropriate locations.

2. Behavior

> Dog does not solicit attention, visit, or annoy any member of the general public.

> Dog does not disrupt the normal course of business.

> Dog does not vocalize unnecessarily, i.e., barking, growling, or whining.

> Dog shows no aggression toward people or other animals.

> Dog does not solicit or steal food or other items from the general public.

3. Training

> Dog is specifically trained to perform three or more tasks to mitigate aspects of the client's disability.

> Dog obeys the commands of the client, except in cases of intelligent disobedience. (An example of intelligent disobedience, which is an advanced assistance dog behavior, is when a blind partner tells her guide dog to take her across the street but the dog sees traffic approaching and refuses to go.)

> Dog works calmly and quietly on harness, leash, or other tether.

> Dog is able to perform its tasks in public.

> Dog must be able to lie quietly beside the handler without blocking aisles, doorways, etc.

> Dog is trained to urinate and defecate on command.

> Dog stays within twenty-four inches of its handler at all times unless the nature of a trained task requires it to be working at a greater distance.

These guidelines don't sound particularly tough or complicated. They simply describe a companion dog with good manners who is under the control of her handler. Aside from the reference to intelligent disobedience, the guidelines mention requirements for only the most basic canine social skills: Don't annoy people or other animals, don't eliminate when and where you're not supposed to, don't offend others with your bad hygiene, and don't create havoc wherever you go.

If you own a dog who acts this way, you have a very pleasant canine companion—even if she doesn't know "stay" from "heel." What she does know is how to behave nicely as your companion in public.

A couple of years ago, my husband and I had a garage sale at our suburban home in northern Virginia. Early on a sunny Saturday morning, we brought out our sale items and placed them in front of our garage and along our driveway. Soon the serious shoppers arrived, and later families visited at a more leisurely pace. A young couple walked up the driveway accompanied by a toddler in a stroller and their dog on a leash. The dog was calm and appeared to be under control. However, while the couple looked at our items for sale, their dog walked up to a television set we had placed on the driveway, lifted her leg, and peed generously. I was horrified and pointed out the infraction to the dog's owners. The father was apologetic, but commented that it was a "male dog thing" over which he had no control.

Relieving yourself in the human environment without regard to propriety is not a "male dog thing." It's a poorly socialized dog thing.

WHAT AN ASSISTANCE DOG IS

Last spring I sat in an indoor café having lunch with Lydia Wade-Driver, the executive director of Blue Ridge Assistance Dogs (BRAD) in Manassas, Virginia. I was concluding my two-day visit to her training facility. Of course, our outing included the company of one of her assistance dogs, Aria, an experienced yellow Labrador Retriever and a permanent resident of BRAD. Aria is a former brood bitch who now acts as the school's demonstration dog and Lydia's helper. Lydia sometimes uses Aria to train the spouse or parent of a partner how to handle an assistance dog.

The presence of a dog in a public place, especially one "dressed" in her assistance dog vest, always attracts attention. I noticed many people watching the three of us and commenting to their friends.

After we had finished our lunch and were chatting over a cup of coffee, several customers approached us and told Lydia enthusiastically what a "very nice" dog she had. But all Aria had done was to enter the café, wait next to us while we ordered our lunch, walk with us to our table, and lie quietly beside us while we ate our meal. Aria didn't perform a single behavior on command the entire time we were there. One man, who was working on his laptop nearby, paused to say that it was all he could do "not to get up and pet that dog" because he could see she was such a "nice" dog.

Aria joins us for lunch.

What was it about Aria that had enthralled so many people? It certainly wasn't her repertoire of funny tricks or helpful behaviors. Without her vest, she was really quite ordinary, at least in her appearance. But her demeanor was quite extraordinary; how many of the customers in the café could name a single dog they knew who was capable of acting so "nicely" in the same situation? Not many, I'm sure.

We would all like to own a "nice" dog, but what does that term mean, exactly? (I'd like to offer the definition "does not pee on my possessions" for consideration, but I know it means much more than that!) Using today's positive, reward-based training methods, owners can develop a training plan to teach their dogs specific behavioral skills such as "sit" or "lie down" or "fetch." But it's more difficult to develop a training program with the goal of producing a "nice" dog. Specifically, what kinds of skills does a dog need to be "nice" while in the company of humans and other dogs?

Assistance dog trainers have shown me the specific qualities of an assistance dog that define our picture of a "nice," well-socialized companion dog. They know the specific skills that make Aria, and dogs like her, such "nice" dogs. They are the social and emotional skills that result from proper socialization, and I've described them in the remainder of this chapter. Once we identify and understand these canine skills, we can, with the trainers' help, plan a socialization program targeted at developing them in our own dog.

We will keep this picture in mind as we establish the techniques and goals of the socialization training program.

Reliable

It's not very helpful for a partner to own an assistance dog who, when asked to perform a behavior, offers the canine equivalent of "maybe later." When you are having an asthma attack and ask your assistance dog to bring your inhaler to you, you don't want to say afterwards, "She does it fine at home, but I couldn't get her to do it in a hotel room." A dog may know how to perform a specific behavior, but the ability to offer it reliably, no matter the circumstances, is a hallmark of an assistance dog.

There are different types of reliability owners can instill in their dogs. One type is a result of the dog's fear of the consequences if she fails to comply. These consequences sometimes come in the form of harsh treatment or physical punishment. For instance, an owner might order her dog to lie down in the house or the car or the veterinarian's waiting room. If the dog does not comply, the owner might jerk on the dog's choke collar or yell at the dog or even push her down. It's not pleasant to be on the receiving end of this type of treatment. So to avoid it, the dog will perform the behavior most of the time, unless the situation is so distracting that she just can't think straight at that moment. For instance, the vet's office may be so full of distracting sights, sounds, other animals, and unfamiliar people that the dog may temporarily forget about the consequences of a lack of compliance as she tries to deal with the overwhelming environment.

Our overall mental picture of this type of dog suggests a wary animal who is nervous when away from home. She looks for ways to avoid human interaction because she may become distracted, make a mistake, and suffer the unpleasant consequences. This dog hesitates to try learning a new behavior because it only leads to new possibilities of making a mistake. She often looks away from her owner, hoping that the owner won't notice her and give her a signal, because the chain of events that follows a signal is not usually very pleasant.

Another type of reliability results from the dog's desire to offer a requested behavior anywhere because of the positive consequences, in the form of rewards, associated with doing so. Assistance dogs blossom at the opportunity to work, which means they must be ready to respond to a variety of signals in many different locations. Just before Lydia and I took Aria to lunch with us, the dog became eager and attentive when Lydia dressed her for the upcoming working trip. Aria had no idea where she was going or what she would be asked to do, but she was enthusiastic about the trip and the chance to work.

A dog who has experienced the rewards of compliance, such as a treat or a game of fetch, is off to a good start to happily offering requested behaviors. A dog who has been taught to handle the distracting sights, sounds, other animals, and unfamiliar people found in new environments has developed the composure required to offer those behaviors reliably.

Our overall mental picture of this type of dog suggests an animal who is looking for opportunities to display her learned behaviors in exchange for a much anticipated reward. The dog will try a new behavior in the hope of finding another way in which to receive rewards. She watches her owner for signs of a pending interaction—a chance to win a reward. However, she doesn't pester her owner if the owner communicates the need for a quiet demeanor. Different environments don't get in the way of her performance because she has developed the social skills to handle them and still remain responsive. Assistance dogs typify this type of reliability.

Self-Disciplined

Marilyn Wilson, the head staff trainer at the St. Francis of Assisi Service Dog Foundation in Roanoke, Virginia, has experience with dog training from all angles. She occasionally teaches an obedience class for the public, offers dog tracking classes with her husband, and manages the assistance dog training program for the foundation.

Marilyn's Thursday evening Puppy Raiser class sometimes meets at the Valley View Mall, an indoor upscale shopping center in Roanoke. The mall manager has invited the foundation to meet there for puppy socialization training. I came along one night to watch. The group of six young, future assistance dogs and their trainers gathered in a quiet corner of the mall's lower level to talk about their training experiences the previous week with each other and with Marilyn. Then, each puppy raiser took a turn walking her puppy down one of the busy mall corridors, in front of the stores and among the shoppers, rewarding the puppy for good behavior in the highly stimulating environment of the busy mall.

"How would you describe a self-disciplined dog?" I asked Marilyn during a break in the training. "That's easy," she answered. "First, think of a dog who is not self-disciplined. That's a dog whose motto is, 'If I can do it, I will do it.' That dog has no impulse control at all. The only thing stopping her from doing just about anything that occurs to her is the physical restraint placed on her by her owner. If she spots another dog while on a walk, she dashes after it. Only the owner's firm hold on her leash prevents her from confronting the other dog. When the front door swings open, she bolts through it unless her owner blocks her path.

"The self-disciplined dog has learned and incorporated additional criteria into her judgment. She has added the question, 'Should I do it?' to her decision-making. Most people don't train their dogs how to develop any judgment on their own. They physically manage their dogs at every step, avoiding the need for the dog to learn or demonstrate self-discipline. It's exhausting and dangerous because the owner can never let down their guard."

While on a walk, the self-disciplined dog refers back to her social skills training and decides not to try to chase another dog because her owner has trained her to remain with them unless she is released. The dog may require a gentle reminder, such as her owner saying "stay with me" in a soft voice when they notice that she has spotted another dog. But the leash is not the primary control tool. When the front door opens, the self-disciplined dog looks to her owner for direction: "Are we going outside together now?" A body block from the owner is not the primary control tool. Thus, the socially adept dog demonstrates the significance of *self* in the word "self-discipline."

Now let's look at another aspect of canine self-discipline that goes beyond the ability to offer a variety of behaviors in a variety of settings. True self-discipline is a deeper skill than the ability to resist tempting behaviors when you know you shouldn't indulge in them. It's also the emotional skill of maintaining self-control in a variety of life situations. As my friend's daughter would say, "Can you just not freak out, please?"

Self-control does not mean disinterested or aloof. Assistance dogs are full of energy and greet each day with happy anticipation of new and stimulating adventures. Self-controlled dogs are not dull dogs, they are dogs who can pace themselves in their reactions to situations while still enjoying themselves. A self-disciplined dog can:

- Remain calm in any environment, even when it's escalating in intensity
- Play with restraint and good manners with people of all ages, with other dogs, with puppies, and with other animals, and stop playing when she receives an indication that the game is over
- Listen to her owner in unfamiliar settings
- Relax and settle down when she's away from home
- Ignore items, people, and animals that she has been asked to avoid
- Abstain from getting involved in an exciting event when her owner has cautioned her not to do so
- Disengage when required

Sound a bit inhibited? It may, at first. But, think of the many opportunities your dog will have to travel with you, play with you, and become your everyday companion if she has these social skills. Then think of how often you will have to leave her at home if she cannot conduct herself with some self-control and in a socially acceptable way. After all, *you* have to exhibit these social skills in order to participate in the human environment. People who cannot control themselves in a social setting soon become unwelcome.

Years ago, one of my co-workers volunteered as a middle school soccer referee. During one game, he was hit on the side of his head with a purse by a mother who had raced onto the field, enraged with one of his calls in a close game. My friend later described her to me as "like a wild-eyed dog that had slipped her leash." That lady should refer to the first bullet point on page 21 if she wants to continue to attend soccer games.

Assistance dog trainers know that a wheelchair-bound partner cannot physically stop their dog from picking up a cigarette butt on the ground. Nor can they run after the dog if she breaks free and chases a rabbit. Self-control is not an option for an assistance dog; it's a necessity.

While watching Marilyn Wilson and her puppy raisers at the mall, it occurred to me that assistance dogs are held to an even higher standard of self-discipline than most people. Strangers of all ages, including young children, were approaching the assistance dog teams-in-training. Children were grabbing and hugging the pups, people were petting them and blocking their path, disinterested people were lightly bumping the pups with their shopping bags as they passed by, and some of the kids started following closely behind the pups. The pups' personal space was being violated left and right. If a stranger approached *me* in the mall and hugged me or started following on my heels, I definitely *would* freak out, and to hell with social skills and self-control! But an assistance dog has to find the resoluteness within herself to endure it.

Most family dogs live their lives under highly controlled conditions. They live in a house, run in a fenced yard, walk on a leash, travel in a car, eat when fed, eliminate when let outdoors. They make few decisions for themselves. They have not developed the skill of consulting their own mind when presented with a possibility. Their owners forget to teach them the self-discipline they can tap into when they remove the dog from the confines of her carefully managed life. When we take a look at most dogs' living conditions, we can see that daily life generally offers few opportunities to teach a dog self-discipline. But dogs do not become properly socialized on their own and without specific instruction.

Assistance dog trainers model self-discipline for the dogs through their own behavior. When training in private and in public, they conduct themselves in a pleasant and appropriate manner and always remain mentally connected with the dogs. It's no wonder to me that the dogs catch on so fast, because the trainers don't ask for more from the dogs than they give. The trainers are a calm, soft-spoken bunch who don't indulge in exaggerated outward manifestations of frustration, impatience, or excitability. They are bright, enthusiastic, and highly invested in the relationship they have with the dogs. They ask the same in return, and they get it.

As companion dog owners, if we give our dog the gift of learned self-discipline, if we guide our dog's ability to manage her own behavior by using her social skills training, we will receive an even greater gift in return: a take-anywhere canine companion whose company is one of life's greatest pleasures.

Careful

As I look around at a typical group of ten beginning obedience class students and their dogs, I watch the animals closely. I could describe the judgment processes of most of them as "ready, fire, aim." The dogs maintain a very high level of arousal—they are on a hair trigger. They respond to even moderate stimuli while in class, such as a noise or the presence of another dog, instantly and vigorously. Their display requires the intervention of their owner to correct. Afterward, the dogs assess the situation with a look on their faces that seems to say, "What just happened?"

If you watch an assistance dog respond to moderate stimuli, you might just barely be able to detect the split second of thinking that passes before the dog takes action. I watched a group of assistance dog staff trainers at St. Francis of Assisi all working at the same time with the dogs. The dogs were in the advanced stage of their training. A couple of the trainers told their dogs to lie down. Other trainers started throwing a tennis ball around the room to the two or three dogs who were not lying down. Of course, each trainer had her eye on her own dog. The downed dogs watched their trainers and the flying tennis balls, evaluating whether they were allowed to play. They stayed in place. The playing dogs watched the tennis balls carefully, and each dog only retrieved her own ball. If another dog's tennis ball flew by the nose of one of the dogs, I could see her stop for a millisecond, recognize that the ball did not belong to her, and look again for her ball. Later, the dogs switched places, and the dogs who had been on a down-stay got to play. Although they were all highly aroused, each dog inserted a moment of time to consider her behavior before acting. *Their* judgment followed the progression "ready, aim, (think), fire."

In his book about human psychology, *Blink*, Malcolm Gladwell refers to this type of thinking as "inserting white space." White space, in this context, means the miniscule moment of consideration needed to make a good judgment about your impending behavior. He says that when we do not insert white space, the result is what he calls "mind blindness." A person suffering from mind blindness has been stressed to the point where they forget to insert white space in their thinking when under pressure and make a snap, low-quality decision about what to do next. People start to make mistakes they later regret. They stop relying on the input they are receiving from the environment and revert to action without consideration.

Gladwell identifies the elements that foster the skill of inserting white space into the thinking process as training and experience. Think about the different ways an experienced police officer and an ordinary citizen might react at the scene of an armed robbery at a convenience store. The citizen might scream, cry, or bolt for the door, thereby attracting a bullet. The police officer, especially if he was handling the scene on his own so he could insert a millisecond of white space into the process, might find cover and wait for a clear shot at the robber. The policeman's default behavior in a stressful environment is to insert the white space needed in his thinking to make a high-quality decision about his next move. Contrary to the citizen, his training and experience have installed this default behavior into his psychology.

Now, let's say the citizen happens to be an accomplished pianist and the policeman plays the piano as a hobby. Which person do you suppose would think more clearly when performing on the stage for a full house at Carnegie Hall? Which person would be able to insert a bit of white space into their thinking in *that* environment before they acted?

So inserting white space is learned through training and experience and can become a default behavior if it is practiced well enough. It does not start out as a general skill. But the good news is, if it's practiced many times and in many circumstances, it becomes easier and faster to learn for each particular circumstance.

Assistance and therapy dogs have been trained to think before they act. They have been taught the skill of inserting a split second of white space into their thinking. They have developed the habit of taking input from their trainers even in a stressful environment. They have become careful. A careful dog does not lose sight of the need to keep extracting information from the environment before acting, even when the pressure increases. She steps up to make her own decision about what to do next unless directed otherwise by her handler.

Let's not get too abstract about carefulness. Careful dogs do not know "right" from "wrong." They do know which reactions earned them benefits in the past and which reactions didn't. Careful dogs learn to modulate their behavior based on perceived consequences, not on morality.

A careful dog is a pleasure to be around. She's trustworthy, and you don't lose that invisible connection you have with her when the environment heats up. She's learned a valuable life skill.

Able to Change Focus Easily

Participating in the sport of dog agility has helped me understand and appreciate the importance of teaching a dog to smoothly shift her focus. Assistance dogs regularly make use of this important skill, as well.

At an agility trial, the off-leash dog must run a course consisting of about twenty obstacles, including tunnels, bar jumps, an A-frame, a teeter-totter, a raised dog walk, and others. Each agility judge designs and sets up a different course at each trial. The handler first familiarizes herself with each course by walking it without her dog. Then the handler and dog run the course together. The handler must guide her dog through the course with a combination of voice and hand signals, and body language cues.

The dog's environment consists of a square piece of geography of about 100 feet by 100 feet that is filled with obstacles. The dog must run from one obstacle to another in the correct order and must complete each one properly. She must see each jump and hurdle it; she must identify the dog walk and balance herself as she negotiates its up ramp, its cross board, and its down ramp; she must find the opening to the tunnel and dash through it. But the only member of the team who knows the order in which to take each obstacle on the course is the handler. So the dog also must focus on the handler's signals to determine the correct path from one obstacle to another. From the dog's point of view, the ability to easily transition between focusing on her handler and focusing on her environment is critical to completing the courses without incurring scoring faults, such as taking the wrong jump at the wrong time.

In the sixty seconds or so that it takes the team to run the course, the successful dog has shifted her focus deftly between her environment (the obstacles) and her handler many times. She has negotiated each obstacle while listening to and watching her handler for signals about where to run next. Dogs who get too caught up in the excitement of negotiating the obstacles and who forget to mentally check in with their handlers for direction will miss parts of the course and fail to qualify. Dogs who just want to run along close to their owners as if they are on a short, invisible leash will also miss obstacles because they are too focused on their handler and don't see the obstacles. That's why agility handlers spend a lot of time teaching their dogs to make transitions of focus skillfully.

Assistance dog trainers incorporate the same kind of training into their programs. Think about the assistance dog who accompanied the student in a wheelchair at George Mason University. The dog walked next to his partner from the parking area to the campus while watching out for the busy vehicle traffic (environment focus). When they approached the curb, the partner asked her dog to help pull her wheelchair up the apron from the street to the sidewalk (handler focus). Once under way on the sidewalk, the dog calmly accompanied his partner several blocks to the student union building (environment focus). Once inside, the partner stopped in the snack shop where she asked the dog to give her payment to the cashier (handler focus). The dog waited under her table while his partner ate a snack (environment focus), then responded to his partner when she asked the dog to throw her empty drink cup in the trash (handler focus). They proceeded to class together, including taking an elevator (environment focus). In class, the partner asked her dog to pick up her dropped pen (handler focus).

What would have happened if the assistance dog had been totally unaware of the traffic swirling around them in the parking lot and the partner had to manage her dog closely as well as negotiate her way through the area? Or if the dog had become so distracted by the traffic that the partner could not get her dog's attention when she wanted her dog to help pull her up the sidewalk apron? What if the presence of all the students in the classroom had so distracted the dog that the partner could not get her dog to respond to her signal to pick up the dropped pen?

Assistance dog trainers cultivate the dog's ability to make multiple, graceful transitions between a focus on the owner and a focus on the environment. Just like people, assistance dogs must be able to shift focus depending on where the circumstances of the moment require their attention.

Most of the dogs entering the beginner training classes I have taught have either a strong handler focus or a strong environment focus, but have great difficulty transitioning between the two. The handler-focused dog becomes nervous at the approach of another person or dog. She shows distress, especially in a classroom setting and when separated from her owner. She has difficulty playing games that require distance from the owner, such as fetch a ball, and has trouble responding to "stay" when the owner leaves her side.

The environment-focused dog spends most of her time at the end of her leash and with her back end facing her owner. She tries to greet the other dogs in the class and accost the other handlers and visitors in the classroom. The owner can't get the dog to look at them or even take a treat from them because she's so stimulated and distracted by the environment. The only control the handler can exert over the dog is physical restraint. In my experience, this type of dog dominates the ranks of beginner obedience class dogs.

Although dogs may start out with a propensity for one type of focus or another, assistance dogs must learn how to move between both types in order to do their jobs. Assistance dog trainers work on this canine social skill until it becomes second nature for the dog and focus can easily be directed by signals from the handler when required.

Many owners who can't seem to get their dog's attention when they're away from home repeat themselves, raise their voices, or try to up the ante and make the rewards of compliance more attractive to their dog. If their dog pays attention to them, the dog will get a "high value" reward, such as cheese, which she will not receive just for sitting when asked. Those solutions are appropriate to use in an obedience class, where there aren't many other options. Primarily, you are there to teach behaviors, not to teach socialization. But these methods are temporary Band-Aids applied to allow an inadequately socialized dog to get through a single obedience class. They're not a replacement for socialization training itself.

Why is the ability to shift focus useful to a companion dog? Because in order to develop a pleasant, take-anywhere dog, you must be able to direct her behavior with something other than brute force and your dog cannot take directional cues from you if new environments, objects, people, or animals cancel her ability to concentrate on your signals. An anxious dog who is uncomfortable anywhere other than right beside her owner cannot be left alone in a motel room or the guest room at your Aunt Jenny's house and might snap at other dogs who approach in a friendly manner.

A lack of socialization accounts for much of a dog's inability to target and transition her focus properly.

A dog who has been socialized to complex environments will not require higher-value rewards to adjust her focus where her owner directs. The environment will hold interest but is not a mesmerizing attraction for this dog. In the socialized dog's eyes, the owner is not the person who prevents the dog from fully indulging in the environment. They are the person who allows the dog greater access to the environment as a result of their successful partnership. This ungrudging, cheerful willingness to switch focus between the interesting, inviting environment and the requirements of the handler is a hallmark of an assistance dog.

Trainers also cultivate in assistance dogs the ability to shift focus from one handler to another. The dogs spend their first weeks with their littermates and breeder, then a puppy raiser takes over for several months, then a couple of staff trainers work with the dog for awhile, and then the dog is placed with her partner. In addition, some pups have spent time in a shelter, or the pup may enter a "prison pups" program where prisoners help raise future assistance dogs. A puppy sitter may keep the pup while the puppy raiser travels where dogs are not allowed.

Family dogs benefit when they can skillfully transition from one handler to another. They should be comfortable with all family members, visitors, friends, the veterinarian, and pet sitters. At agility trials, I have held the leash of dogs getting ready to run a course while their owners put away the dog treats, grabbed some water, or checked the running order sheet. I have held the leash of beginner dogs in class while their owners replenished their treat pouches, ran back to the car for their water bottle, or used a poop bag to clean up outside the building.

Some dogs cannot tolerate even a few minutes away from their owner, bringing much needless anxiety into their lives. The cure: positive-outcome socialization.

Confident

During an assistance dog's career, she may move to a different state or even to a different country. She might live in a house and then move to an apartment. Her partner's health may decline, and the dog may be required to learn additional skills to further assist them. Her partner may work at several jobs, each requiring the dog to assimilate into a new workplace. Her partner may adopt a stray kitten or other pet. But her partner cannot go back to the assistance dog trainer and say, "I'd like to trade Queenie in for an apartment-type assistance dog now." Assistance dogs must remain open and eager to engage in lifelong learning. Therefore, their trainers help them develop the social skill that reinforces this cooperative and enthusiastic attitude: confidence. "A confident dog is smart, but also versatile and adjustable," says Lydia Wade-Driver of BRAD.

A confident dog is not a brash dog, impertinent and sometimes rude. A confident dog is self-assured and poised, free from doubt or reluctance. She is not afraid to try new things because her previous attempts, whether correct or not, have been treated by her trainers as learning opportunities and not as successes or failures. The trainers find ways to guide the dog rather than punish her; to reward her rather than deprive her; to encourage her rather than dominate her.

An assistance dog must learn a number of particular behaviors quickly and then get on with her job. She will have a lot of tasks to perform, and she must perform them correctly. The trainer must do the work efficiently and be ready to take on the next group of assistance dogs awaiting attention.

And that's why confidence is so important. In an assistance dog's training schedule, there's no time for a dog who always hesitates or holds back because of a lack of confidence. Positive-outcome socialization builds up a dog's natural inclination to work with humans. It prevents disintegration of the dog's willingness, based upon negative past experiences, to try new behaviors or try interacting with new animals, people, things, or places.

When Karen Hough brought Jane for her training session at PetSmart, I watched as Karen took Jane from the car and gave her a few seconds to gather herself and determine where she was. Then they set off for the store. As they approached the automatic doors, a store employee pushing a large, noisy flat-bed trolley ran up right behind them and followed them closely through the door. Jane noticed the trolley, but she didn't panic. You could see her make the effort to collect herself. Karen, with eyes in the back of her head (as all assistance dog trainers seem to have), praised Jane after they had entered the store.

"That was not a planned challenge," Karen explains. "But it's just as important for handlers to reward unplanned events that your dog handles well as it is to reward planned training events. Jane knows I'm always watching her and will catch even her unintended successes. She knows I'm always aware of the environment surrounding her and I'm always there to reward her and to help her, if needed."

When a dog is certain that she will always have a portion of her owner's attention, even when she is not engaged in a specific training or play exercise, and when she feels this constant connection, she relaxes and develops that very important canine characteristic: confidence.

When Lydia and Aria and I sat in the café having lunch together, I counted at least six times that Lydia glanced over the edge of the tabletop and looked directly into Aria's eyes for about one second. It was an extremely subtle thing—no more than a shifting of the eyes—and I had to concentrate to catch it. Several times Lydia was speaking to me when she glanced at Aria, but she never skipped a beat in her conversation when she briefly connected with Aria. Each time she looked down at Aria, the dog seemed to know the glance was coming, because she lifted her head very slightly and returned Lydia's direct glance.

I'm describing a few microscopic moments, but, to me, they held monumental significance. With her eyes, Lydia was saying, "I'm here with you, Aria, even though I'm otherwise occupied. Nothing can happen that I'm not aware of." And Aria was answering, "I know you're here for me. Nothing can go wrong."

Developing confidence in a dog is often forgotten in the effort to train specific behaviors that an owner wants their dog to know. After all, who needs confidence when your actions are managed completely by your handler and you don't need to exert any self-control or make any decisions? But confidence ranks high on the list of attributes required in a working assistance dog. They must complete tasks and control their reactions to unplanned events. Their partners are not capable of completely managing them. Both partner and dog must depend on each other.

Owners of companion dogs can discover the fringe benefit of confidence building with their dogs. A canine with self-confidence is not *less* connected with her owner, she's *more* connected than the average dog. Confidence doesn't develop when a dog learns to do things on her own, without your input; it develops from her trust that you will always be there to support her, so she can freely do her work as trained, have a fun playtime, step onto an escalator, or stay quietly in a motel room. It is an invisible connection that is stronger than a leash, and it is a hallmark of an assistance dog.

Responsible

A profound change takes place in a dog who, with the help of her trainer, has developed reliability, self-discipline, carefulness, the ability to change focus, and confidence. The dog understands that she has a personal responsibility for her own actions. Her owner is not the person who dictates her actions at every moment and in every situation. Her owner monitors and supports her actions. Her actions no longer depend on the application or removal of various physical restraints by her owner, such as leashes and baby gates. Her actions depend on her own judgment, based on her training and on information provided to her at the moment by her owner through verbal signals or other means of communication.

Based upon her experiences with her owner during training, she knows that her owner will remember that she is, after all, just a dog, and will not ask her to perform outside of the limits of her capabilities. But within those limits, the dog-owner relationship is a partnership to which the dog brings responsibility for her behaviors and reactions. She is your true partner and a capable inhabitant of the human environment, physically and mentally.

WHAT AN ASSISTANCE DOG IS NOT

Before we finish painting our mental picture of what an assistance dog *is*, let's briefly think about what an assistance dog *isn't*.

An assistance dog is not a robot or a machine. Although our description of an assistance dog paints a picture of a beautifully socialized and trained helper, an almost perfect companion, assistance dogs are really just dogs. They make mistakes, their skills fade without follow-up training, and they occasionally balk at performing a task for a reason unknown at the time. They might knock over the trash when left alone.

An assistance dog is not a babysitter or a medical caregiver. Although an assistance dog may alert a mother to the onset of her child's seizure, an assistance dog is not expected to medically monitor a child's health. Although an assistance dog may bring an asthma inhaler to her partner, she is not expected to offer, independently, such caregiving behavior without a signal from her partner. Assistance dogs are not asked to be more than a dog.

An assistance dog is not a security or protection animal. Some physically disabled people feel insecure and want a dog for personal protection. Certainly, just having a dog makes many people feel more secure. However, aggression and assistance dogs don't mix.

An assistance dog is not a specially bred Labrador Retriever or Lab cross. Successful assistance dogs come in all sizes, breeds, and mixes. Some are bred for their work, and others are rescued from a shelter or donated to an assistance dog training program.

ASSISTANCE DOG TRAINERS

Now it's time to take a look at the trainer standing next to the assistance dog in our mental picture. What are the hallmarks of an assistance dog trainer?

Truthfulness

I once watched a novice handler running her dog in an agility competition. About halfway through the course, the handler told the dog to run through a tunnel. The dog hesitated and wouldn't go through it. The handler told the dog again to go through, but received the same response. She became exasperated. Then, she said, excitedly, "Go get the cookie in the tunnel!"

Of course, there was no cookie in the tunnel, because treats are not permitted on an agility course. The dog did race into the tunnel, but I will never forget the look on her face when she exited. Her owner had told her a lie. There was no cookie in the tunnel.

That dog is an advanced agility competitor now, but her speed and accuracy has fluctuated rather than increased. And her tunnel time is slow.

Assistance dog trainers know lots of tricks and shortcuts, but never lie to their dogs. An assistance dog trainer knows that too much is sacrificed for the sake of expediency when you tell your dog a "little white lie" to get her to do something in the moment. Assistance dog trainers build trust on a solid foundation of truthfulness.

Anticipation

Assistance dog trainers don't merely react to a dog's behavior, correcting it if it's wrong. They monitor the environment, predict what's coming, and anticipate their dog's reaction. They use the environment to teach the dog, but they've got to read it in advance to do so.

Karen Hough knew that Jane would stay calm in PetSmart while in the company of the employees and shoppers, but the presence of another dog would cause Jane to break concentration. Karen didn't wait for Jane to notice another dog, demonstrate a break in her composure, and then correct the dog. Karen saw another dog approaching and said softly to Jane "Easy, steady, steady. Good job. Good job," before the encounter ever took place. The dog held her ground with complete decorum until the other dog had passed.

Linda Eaton, also a staff trainer at Saint Francis of Assisi, told me, "We try to get value out of every moment." That's possible only when the handler can see the moment coming.

Focus on the Dog

Whether the trainers were talking with me, teaching a class, eating a meal, or walking to their car, they always had an eye on their dog.

I watched Marilyn Wilson conduct a puppy-raiser training class in a hotel meeting room, with puppy raisers and dogs practicing all kinds of social skills and behaviors for an hour. She brought one of the mature assistance dogs, Caesar, to the class. Caesar creeps forward in tiny increments, always trying to get a little closer to Marilyn. But Marilyn wants him to learn to stay put. Even while she was orchestrating the classroom hullabaloo of a group of young pups and their handlers in constant motion, she sensed every time Caesar even thought about starting to inch his way out from under a table and reminded him to remain in position.

I was seated right beside Caesar, and I could see the subtle indications that he was planning to try to decrease the real estate between him and Marilyn. But Marilyn was always a step ahead of him. Assistance dog trainers really do have eyes in the backs of their heads!

Predictability

One of the greatest gifts assistance dog trainers give to the dogs is their own predictability. After watching the trainers in action, I found that they use body language signals, word cues, toys, and other training tools such as clickers in the same way almost all the time.

Even more important than the predictability of the trainers' physical actions is the predictability of the emotional responses of the trainers. They do not scold a dog for something she did one day and make no comment the next time the dog does the same thing. They don't call the dog to them when they are relaxed, but grab the dog and pull her along when they are in a hurry. They don't rush her through her training when they don't feel well. They just don't train that day.

Handling a dog in this way requires self-discipline on the part of the trainer. But an amazing sense of relaxation descends over a dog whose owner is predictable to her, physically and emotionally. More than once, Karen Hough has reminded me, "Dog training is more about managing the owner's behavior than it is about managing the dog's behavior."

Everyday People

Assistance dog trainers have spouses, children, hobbies, and social commitments. Puppy raisers have jobs and families and even other pets, just as we do. They don't have a lot of spare time to struggle with elaborate, time-consuming dog training programs. The puppy raisers have to turn in a well-socialized and trained puppy, ready for task training, in less than a year. The trainers have only about four to six months to spend on task training before assigning the dog to a partner. The time devoted to training is measured in weeks and months, not years. Certainly, the average dog owner can accomplish good socialization training with their dog in the personal time they have available.

Of course, assistance dog trainers are everyday people, but they are not ordinary trainers. They are quite extraordinary trainers, and they can show us how to become better trainers for our companion dogs.

Chapter 3

From Domestication to Behavior Modification to Socialization

DOMESTICATION: WE FIND THE KEY

Domestication is the process by which an animal or a plant adapts to an existence in close association with humans. Domestication is a tool that has enabled us to develop a reliable food supply, transportation, security, and companionship while being less subject to the whims of climate and other environmental factors. For instance, keeping herds of domesticated animals, such as cows and pigs, for their meat replaced the need to hunt for difficult-to-find, free-ranging sources of meat. Using animals for transportation, such as horses and camels, reduced the need to walk long distances and endure severe environmental conditions to travel, fish, or hunt. Growing cultivated crops eliminated the need to scavenge for nutritious plant foods.

The domestication of the dog represents the first known instance of the domestication of an animal or plant. The company of canines offered security from the threats of wild predators (and probably other humans) and provided the pleasures of companionship with an agreeable member of the animal kingdom.

Controversy surrounds scientific estimates of when dogs were first domesticated. Most scientists believe dogs are descended from wild wolves; the fact that they are still able to interbreed with wolves supports this view. Wolf and human remains have been discovered together dating from as early as 400,000 years ago. But the divergence of the wild wolf and the domestic dog is shrouded in the mists of history. Based on archaeological and skeletal evidence, researchers believe dogs diverged from wolves about 15,000 years ago in East Asia, but more recent genetic and DNA studies suggest that the domestication of the dog may have occurred earlier. No matter when this fortuitous event took place, the dog indeed has adapted to a life lived in close association with humans.

The domestication of an animal differs from the process of taming an animal in that domestication alters the physiology and the behavior of the animal at the genetic level. A *tame* animal retains his wild genetic makeup but has been habituated to the company of humans. Taming results from a learning process that affects only the tamed animal of the species. Each subsequent generation of that animal must be tamed again to overcome the inherent wildness. For instance, if you hand raise a baby squirrel from infancy and habituate him to humans, you still have to go through the same taming process, from the beginning, with any of his offspring. In other words, a baby squirrel born to a tamed squirrel will retain his individual wildness, and you will have to tame the baby.

The offspring of a domesticated animal is born with the predisposition to a close association with humans, which is reflected in his behavioral characteristics, genetic makeup, and even physical features. Domestication results from purposeful, selective breeding for these traits. It is directed by humans; the traits do not arise from learning. Wolves born in captivity and raised by humans don't develop a close association with those humans, but merely display a tolerance for the presence of people. Stray or feral dogs, living without a human owner but still genetically domestic animals, can come to accept humans much more readily than wolves who have spent their lives in captivity.

The seminal study about the effects of domestication on wild animals began in 1959 at the Institute of Cytology and Genetics of the Russian Academy of Science. Geneticist Dmitry Belyaev selectively bred wild foxes to favor one specific behavioral characteristic—friendliness to people. After breeding more than twenty generations of foxes, the researchers noticed that significant changes in the animals' behavior and physical makeup were passed down from one generation to another as the animals became friendlier, or more domesticated.

Myrna Milani, a veterinarian and animal behaviorist, has written about the effects of domestication on animal physiology and behavior, including the famous fox study. She says that by the tenth generation, the foxes in the study "were eager to establish human contact, vocalized to attract attention, and sniffed and licked experimenters like pet dogs." Obviously, wild foxes do not display this type of behavior. Future generations of these foxes began to look different than their progenitors. The adults had floppy ears, solid color or piebald coats, shortened muzzles, more prominent eyes, and exhibited monomorphism (males and females looked similar). They also demonstrated a more dependent personality. "The adult foxes retained the physical characteristics of young, immature foxes, a condition known as neotany. Consequently, we can say that domestication freezes the animal in a behaviorally and morphologically immature state," writes Milani.

Young animals quickly begin to respond only to members of their own species and soon develop a fear response to unfamiliar animals, objects, and environments. You might not be shocked if a newborn bunny was willing to approach you during a walk in the woods, but you would be stunned if an adult rabbit did so. We know that all but infant wild animals have no desire to associate closely with humans. This fear reaction ensures the safety of a wild animal in a potentially hostile environment.

However, domestication enlarges and holds open the window that allowed the wild baby rabbit to approach you in the woods. In wild animals, this window is narrow, closes swiftly, and stays locked once it is closed. Domestication prolongs the period of time during which animals can recognize, accept, and bond with other species and with humans. It expands the window of opportunity for habituating to new environments, people, animals, and objects and remains fully open longer. And although it may close at some time, it has no lock.

Humans—who have, in essence, domesticated ourselves to live in close association with other humans—retain many juvenile characteristics into adulthood. Children remain in close association with their parents for many years, often for their entire lives. Humans display a need for touch and bonding throughout their lifetimes—a need most wild animals exhibit only in their youth.

Although domestication alters an animal's physiology and behavioral characteristics, it does not erase the essence of the species. If we believe that dogs are the domesticated version of wolves, we can still see much of the dog's ancient ancestry reflected in his current makeup.

- Territoriality: Wolves designate territories, which they defend. They live in established home territories rather than wander.

- Sense of social order: Wolves exist in cooperative packs with a well-defined hierarchy among the members.

- Ability to communicate complex ideas: Wolves use vocal sounds, scent, and elaborate body postures to communicate information and feelings with others.

- Intelligence: Wolves quickly adjust their behaviors to bring advantage to themselves and their pack.

As it turns out, these inherited characteristics work in favor of the close relationship between people and dogs. Scientists postulate that the basis for the domestication of the dog was a desire for mutual benefit: Ancient humans shared food scraps with wolves to keep them around the camp so the humans could have an early alert to dangers in the environment and the security of protection provided by the presence of the wolves. In the case of dogs, domestication did not result from capture and forced bondage to humans, but originated from a mutual desire for shared benefits.

Our journey with the domestic dog at our side begins with both human and dog as domesticated members of our respective species. The many established and harmonious habits of behavior and emotion we share as a result of our mutual domestication unites us and supports us in our relationship. Few domestic animals find the value in domestication that dogs do. Dogs have discovered the benefits of lifestyle (great food, comfortable living conditions, rewards for compliance), play, interesting activities, and so on that accompany domestication. As the process of domestication continues, our paths grow ever closer and our bonds grow ever stronger.

The prize at the heart of the domestication of companion dogs is the wide window of opportunity it provides for dogs to bond so closely with us. Assistance dog trainers fling open this window and let the whole world of what it means to be the daily companion of a human shine in. The result is a sophisticated companion dog—a dog who's always welcome in human company. It is our challenge to use that wide open window to our greatest advantage as we raise and train our family dogs.

BEHAVIOR MODIFICATION: WE START TO OPEN THE WINDOW

Imagine you are a leader of a Chukchi village in Siberia. The Chukchi were a people who inhabited the area more than 3,000 years ago. They lived in permanent settlements along the frigid coast, hunting and fishing. First you notice that wild dogs hang around your camp waiting to snatch up any scraps of meat or fish left after meals. You notice that the presence of these dogs keeps predators away from your village. The dogs also alert your tribe when predators or strangers approach.

As time passes, the wild dogs become friendlier and more habituated to life at the outskirts of your village. Some villagers hand raise puppies, who become even friendlier. One day, you notice a dog pulling a child along on the snow while the child holds onto his fur. For his efforts, the child throws the dog a meaty bone. The thought crosses your mind that getting a ride to the best fishing grounds several miles from your village might be an improvement over walking. You have just made the leap of thinking from participating in a benign, relatively passive association with these friendly canines to devising ways to modify their behavior to meet your human needs.

But how will you turn the current local pack of rowdy, self-involved dogs into dogs who will actually cooperate and pull a device constructed for human travel on the snow and ice? Watching the dogs as they interact with members of the tribe, you understand that gaining advantage for themselves drives their behavior. A dog will pull the child on the snow if a meaty bone follows the action. The pack of dogs will alert the village of impending danger if they receive enough food scraps to keep them in the vicinity of the village.

So you start with the pups who have been hand raised and who show a stronger inclination to associate with the villagers. You construct a primitive sled that will travel over the snow, and you attach a dog to the sled with a strip of leather. He gets a piece of nice, smelly fish if he just tolerates this treatment. Soon, he learns to appreciate the sled because its presence indicates that a tasty treat is close at hand. But mostly he just stands there, playing around.

You throw the piece of fish out of the dog's reach. He moves to get it, but the sled holds him back. He braces against it and pulls the sled a few feet with him toward the fish. Now you only give the dog the fish when he pulls the sled along.

Fast-forward to a later time when you and the villagers have designed better sleds, have developed a method of hitching the dogs to the sleds, and have established a group of dogs willing to pull them. In fact, you have taken a couple of short trips using the sled pulled by the dogs and now have access to bountiful fishing or hunting grounds previously considered too far to get to from your village.

You have molded the behavior of the dogs to achieve a task—pull a sled in return for a high-quality meal. The dogs want access to this valuable resource, and they have learned to get it by offering this behavior. But some dogs learn the task more easily than others. And you have learned that, when using several dogs to pull a load, the dog in the lead position has to be aware of hazards ahead, such as thin ice or unstable snow, because you are traveling too fast to detect them yourself. The dogs farther back in the group have to pace themselves carefully when the sled makes a turn. These behaviors require more advanced thinking than just pulling forward, and now you cannot direct each action of each dog while under way; each dog must take responsibility for his own actions.

You can mold this more advanced behavior again by providing the dog with advantages and access to resources that are important to him. You can play often and roughly with the lead dog as a reward for his demonstrating assertive behavior. You can allow him to mate with the female dog of his choice. You can teach the other dogs to slow down on your signals for "turn right" and "turn left" by throwing them a chunk of meat when they respond properly.

What you cannot do is attach your dog to a sled and physically force him to pull it long distances or negotiate turns, just as you cannot coerce an assistance dog to pick up a set of dropped keys. Behavior modification isn't about coercion; it's about consequences.

Over time your sled dogs have transformed into the first Siberian Huskies as a result of your selectively breeding dogs who have the physical characteristics to perform their specific work, and they have learned to offer certain behaviors when required in order to obtain a desired resource.

Missing from this equation are words like "love," "devotion," "praise," "spite," and a "desire to please." You did not rely on any of these abstract notions to train your sled dogs to offer a requested behavior when asked. You relied on motivation in the form of scraps of meat, smelly fish tidbits, hearty bones, access to valued sexual partners, and access to rough play to elicit behaviors from your dogs. The dogs give you the behaviors you request, and they receive a perceived advantage.

The sled dogs don't perform their work because they "love" their trainers, and they don't refuse to perform it out of "spite." They evaluate the advantages to themselves, given the situation, and act accordingly. If you have provided the dog with many advantages to performing behaviors requested by you, then you will have trained him to work willingly and even enthusiastically on your behalf. But see if the dog's "love" or "devotion" will keep those behaviors coming forever if you cease to reward them with something the dog perceives as valuable.

It might be romantic to envision a team of sled dogs pulling a Chukchi villager across the snow, executing their task solely out of the loyalty and love they have developed for their owner. But Hollywood created Lassie and Rin Tin Tin in that sentimental image for the entertainment of the public. Real dogs apply themselves to their tasks because they have acquired an affinity for the task as a result of selective breeding by humans and have been trained to offer the desired behaviors through the application of rewards and/or punishments.

This view of dogs as being always on the lookout for an advantage does not diminish the dog-owner relationship at all. In fact, it anchors it in reality and provides you with the tools needed to successfully modify a dog's behavior to accommodate his life with humans. For more than 3,000 years, humans have known how to induce dogs to perform highly complex behaviors when asked, such as working in a team to pull loads under extreme weather conditions. The ancient Chukchi improved their lives immeasurably by using their knowledge of how to modify canine behavior by controlling what the dogs considered valuable assets and bestowing them on the dogs as a reward for work. In doing so, they formed the foundation of one of the most hardworking breeds ever, the Siberian Husky. It makes you wonder why some students in a beginner dog obedience class can't get their dogs to simply lie down when asked.

Domestication provided a window through which humans could visualize a more interactive, mutually beneficial human-canine relationship. Knowledge of canine behavior modification techniques formed the foundation of a broader vision of that relationship. No longer were domesticated dogs useful but passive in their association with humans. Canine behavior modification opened the window to a future of side-by-side work for the mutual benefit of both species.

SOCIALIZATION: WE OPEN WIDE THE WINDOW

During the time of dogs' early association with people, the process of socialization happened in conjunction with the processes of domestication and behavior modification. Siberian Huskies lived in canine groups and often shared shelters with the humans they were closely associated with. They pulled sleds, guarded children, and gave birth in the company of other dogs and humans. Labrador Retrievers lived on ocean-going ships in close contact with their owners and ferried messages from one craft to another. Killing dogs, or weeding them out of the breeding stock, solved problems with dogs who did not socialize or perform well. For instance, a dog who was highly noise sensitive and who often alerted to nothing of consequence quickly became a nuisance and was removed from the group. The dogs who remained after the owner culled the social offenders demonstrated acceptable social skills (learned as an adjunct to their other training) as well as the required behaviors.

When the activity of breeding dogs to be working animals expanded, socialization sometimes took a back seat to refining working skills. If you kept a group of dogs to assist you in hunting game animals, you might house them in a kennel away from your living quarters. You didn't care if they acted pleasantly toward your children or if they indulged in a few dogfights on occasion. These dogs did not participate in your life or even in human society. As long as most of the dogs tolerated your horses, the sound of gunfire, and the company of other dogs on the hunt, they received the rewards of food and the fellowship of others of their own species. Hunt, live in a pack, or face disposal. Not much socialization required there, and its absence was barely missed.

While dogs were trained to perform a wide variety of behaviors, such as herding, hunting, pulling, tracking, and retrieving, regard for any high-level social skill waned. Even so-called companion or lap dogs sometimes demonstrated poor social skills by nipping or snarling at people or not taking to housetraining. The suitability of the dog for a wide variety of tasks came dangerously close to placing him in the category of a tool, rather than a well-socialized companion.

Today, most dogs are unemployed. Modern owners do not require their dogs to perform the work they used to do for us. People travel by car or snowmobile, not by dogsled. People use electronic means of communication; they don't send messages using dogs. People carry sophisticated weapons and have elaborate alarm systems rather than rely on dogs for security. People own herding breeds of dogs who have never seen a sheep and own retrieving breeds who have never had a duck in their mouths.

What do contemporary dog owners want from their animals? Apparently, it's not the physical work they were bred to do. But they do have other work ahead of them: companionship. This is now the chief purpose for owning a dog. Yet what a dilemma we face when we take a dog into our family, only to have him turn out to be a troublesome companion. Now we've made a fifteen-year commitment to a dog who can't accompany us anywhere and sometimes can't even remain in our presence in our own homes because of his lack of social skills.

We resort to obedience training in the hope that we can teach the dog behaviors that will help him become a better companion. But behavioral skills are not the root of what's missing. Social skills are. The role of the contemporary dog has evolved from a working, task-oriented role to a relationship-oriented role, but dog training has not followed and supported this evolution. Traditional dog training still concentrates on teaching tasks to dogs who are greatly in need of social skills.

Actually, humans have achieved some degree of success in fumbling about with undersocialized dogs. We have not thrown up our hands and given up entirely on the dog as a suitable companion just because we can't take him anywhere or allow him to participate fully in family activities due to his lack of social skills. Dogs are naturally friendly, smart animals who eventually figure out a way to fit into the family to the best of their ability. As owners, we resort to close management and an extreme narrowing of the dog's universe to maintain his behavior at socially acceptable levels. We keep him leashed up, tied up, kenneled, confined, baby-gated, barricaded, and even muzzled. We just leave him at home a lot of the time. Although we had in mind a canine companion when we acquired the dog, much of modern dog owning has slipped into an edgy coexistence. The dog has come dangerously close to losing his status as a companion and becoming a mere household pet, like an oversized gerbil.

Assistance and therapy dog owners aim for a higher standard. After all, what good is an assistance dog who can't behave in public? One of the chief purposes of an assistance dog is to enable disabled people to more easily negotiate going out in public. What good is a therapy dog who refuses to ride the hospital elevator or nips a nursing home resident? One of the chief purposes of a therapy dog is to give institutionalized and elderly people reliable access to a well-behaved canine. What good is a companion dog you can't take anywhere because of his inappropriate behavior? One of the chief purposes of a companion dog is to actually accompany you.

Assistance dog trainers carefully distinguish the canine socialization process from the canine behavior modification process. They give the socialization process more weight in their training than they give to behavior modification. They realize that early domestic canines received some satisfactory level of socialization from freely meandering around the campfires of early humans. But human society has become so complex that socialization no longer happens as the natural result of just hanging around. Comprehensive socialization must be undertaken as a separate training step, just as if you were training specific behaviors.

Both behavior training and socialization modify the outward actions of the dog. Behavior training controls outward actions based on the signals of the owner, and social training controls outward actions based on the emotional development of the dog. Only together do these training processes produce a higher standard: the perfect companion dog.

You take for granted that your dog will not know how to sit or lie down at your request until you train him to do so. For help in selecting a method of behavior training that works and feels comfortable to you, you might buy a book about dog training or take your dog to an obedience class where instructors use methods that appeal to you. You patiently learn about signaling your dog, rewarding your dog, play training your dog, maybe you even learn to use a clicker. You practice at home for six or eight weeks and graduate to the next level of beginner training.

But if most owners address socialization at all, they expect that it will occur naturally as a result of taking the dog out to obedience classes and to the park to practice obedience homework. It's the equivalent of only teaching math to school children in the hopes that, in the process of learning math from the verbal instruction of the teacher and interacting verbally with other classmates, the children will pick up enough English language skills to function in human society without actually studying spelling, grammar, composition, or diction. The children might be able to muddle through at some level in the end, but we would not define them as skilled in language. And their life options, resulting from their lack of language skills, would remain severely limited.

These days, socialization training often follows obedience training, thereby making both forms of training more difficult. Assistance dogs learn social skills *before* they learn specific tasks.

The life options of assistance and therapy dogs must be as broad as possible. Who knows where their careers with their owners might take them? And they must be prepared to go.

The life options of a true companion dog also must be as broad as possible. Who knows where your life's journey might take you and your dog? And he, too, must be prepared to go.

Chapter 4

The Right Dog for the Right Role

One morning Marilyn Wilson called me and suggested that I come out to St. Francis of Assisi Service Dog Foundation that afternoon to observe the evaluation of a new puppy. St. Francis wanted to buy a couple of nice puppies to add to their complement of puppies already in the program. A breeder from North Carolina had contacted the foundation about a 20-week-old male yellow Labrador Retriever, who was the only dog still remaining from a recent litter. The pup had a tiny spot with a few black hairs on the top of one of his ears. Although no bigger than the size of a pea, that black spot eliminated him as a candidate for the breed conformation ring because he did not have a perfect yellow coat. The breeder thought the pup might work out as an assistance dog, though, describing him as a large, sturdy, agreeable pup. That's what many assistance dog trainers want for their program.

I arrived at St. Francis moments after the breeder, his wife, and a friend arrived. When a puppy arrives at the foundation for puppy testing, a staff trainer meets the breeder at the car and whisks the puppy into the building. The breeder remains outside, and the trainers start the testing right away. The trainers want to observe the puppy as soon as she arrives, when everything is new to her and she doesn't have her breeder to help or influence her. They don't want the pup to acclimate to the people or the environment of the foundation, even for a few minutes, before they have a chance to evaluate her responses to these entirely new circumstances.

There are many elaborate puppy tests available to dog owners, developed by a wide range of nationally known dog trainers. Puppy and dog training books and the Internet abound with examples of puppy tests and procedures for tabulating and evaluating the responses of the puppies. For this test, Marilyn planned to use a method developed by Suzanne Clothier, a well-respected expert in canine behavior. Clothier's assessment package consists of a description of the exercises to include in the test, how to record the pup's responses, and how to predict the pup's temperament and personality traits within certain guidelines. Marilyn wanted to use this test to get a glimpse of how this pup might work out as an assistance dog.

When I arrived, Marilyn had just brought the pup into the kitchen in the small, single-story house that serves as the administrative center for the foundation. I walked into the room, and there was Beefy, so called by the trainers because, indeed, he was a large, sturdy, handsome male Lab pup, and the first trainer who saw him exclaimed, "Wow, what a beefy boy he is!" However, Beefy was lying flat on the kitchen floor, tucked in a corner against the cabinets, with his head pressed down on his front paws. There were five people in the room: Marilyn, Connie Knisely and Elizabeth Broyles (both staff trainers), me, and Deb (the office manager).

Marilyn stood watching Beefy, perplexed. He absolutely would not move from the corner or even lift his head. He was frozen. She kept her tone of voice low, and all the rest of us kept very still. She only allowed me to take a few pictures without a flash. She brought out a couple of soft toys and a tennis ball and offered them in an inviting way to Beefy. Nothing happened. She opened up a package of string cheese, the canine equivalent of caviar, and offered him a piece. Still no response. She approached him, and he cowered in the corner, head still pressed down. She touched his collar and his leash, and he shrieked and pulled away. The trainers looked at each other with puzzled expressions and then shakes of their heads. When Marilyn attempted to lift Beefy gently to a standing position, he peed on the floor.

Taken aback, Marilyn left the room to have a word with the breeder, who was still waiting outside. She discovered that Beefy had been raised entirely in the breeder's kennel. Before this day, Beefy had never seen a woman—not even the breeder's wife. He had never worn a collar or a leash, had never ridden in a car, and had never walked on a linoleum floor or any surface other than the kennel floor and grass. In fact, he had never been inside a house. He had never been in a crate and was not housetrained. He had not been introduced to interactive toys or received food rewards. Of course, he was "agreeable" to the breeder, who fed him every day. He was a kennel-raised puppy who had been passed over by prospective buyers and now, after twenty weeks of relative

Beefy cowers in a corner and refuses even cheese from Marilyn.

isolation under these conditions, he had experienced all these new things for the first time within the past four hours.

Marilyn suggested that we observe him in the fenced backyard with only herself, Elizabeth, and me present. As soon as Beefy entered the yard, he peed many times, then found the corner where the house met the fence and stayed there. What struck me most was his apparent disregard for the new, friendly people near him. He didn't pay any attention to me, Elizabeth, or Marilyn, except when Marilyn approached him. Then he moved around to maintain a distance of about six feet. Marilyn tried offering toys and the cheese, with no success. She brought out a bowl of water, but Beefy would drink only after Marilyn moved away from it. She sat quietly under a tree for a while, and although it appeared that Beefy might be thinking about investigating her, he stayed out of range. Marilyn and Elizabeth shared disappointed glances.

"There's no way I can even test this puppy," Marilyn said sadly.

I had come to the foundation to witness the administration of a puppy temperament test, and had witnessed instead the pathetic result of a complete lack of socialization in a fine young dog.

After about forty-five minutes, Connie joined us in the yard. The puppy had relaxed a bit, and Connie lay down on the grass under the tree. The rest of us remained on the other side of the yard. After a time, Beefy did come up to Connie and actually stepped over her while she was lying flat on the ground.

But the slightest movement sent Beefy back to the corner of the yard. Eventually, he did take a piece of cheese from Connie. It was one of the saddest things I have ever seen in my time with dogs, and certainly as a former Labrador owner myself, who knows this breed to be highly social, incredibly friendly, accepting of strangers, and quite playful.

Later, Beefy cautiously approaches Marilyn in the yard.

However, my biggest surprise was yet to come. Marilyn carefully picked up Beefy and brought him back into the kitchen. The breeder, embarrassed by Beefy's performance, was saying how much he wished he had done more to socialize Beefy. No kidding!

"We'll take him on probation," Marilyn said. My jaw dropped. After the contracts were signed and the breeder left, Marilyn asked, "Who wants to take Beefy home tonight?" Connie volunteered.

I asked Marilyn why she had agreed to take Beefy. Did she really place so little value on formal puppy testing procedures? "No," she explained, "puppy tests are valuable tools. But when Connie entered the yard, I thought I saw him thinking about connecting with her. He has a couple of traits that will serve an assistance dog well. In the face of extreme stress, he quiets and becomes still. That's better than going wild. He's not too friendly. We want assistance dogs to focus on their partners. He's large boned, so he could help with balance. He's a Labrador, so his good hardwiring is there. And he's a puppy, so we still have time to socialize and test him properly."

I visited St. Francis again just six days after Beefy's arrival. He had been living with Connie, her husband, and their three dogs. He had ventured out and about with Connie, even swimming in a friend's pool. He approached me as soon as he saw me, although he didn't hang around for a lot of petting. He walked around the place comfortably, took cheese from anyone, and didn't pitch a fit when someone pulled on his new collar.

At Connie's house, he had received lavish praise whenever he eliminated outdoors, so his housetraining had improved immensely. Connie laughingly called him "iron bladder." Again, I was stunned.

Beefy eventually investigates Connie.

Whether Beefy will have a career as an assistance dog is still an open question. He wouldn't be my choice for a future agility dog. I want an agility prospect with lots of pizzazz. But handicapped partners don't want that kind of dog. Beefy might be just the right partner for them.

What I learned is that personality profile scores are just one aspect of puppy selection. People tend to feel comforted by an extensive checklist that they can score and then consult to find the right answer. But when you add in gut instinct, personal experience, an understanding of the future role of the dog, and the skill set of the individual trainer, you have an even better recipe for matching the right dog to the right role.

OTHER TRAINERS WEIGH IN

Lydia Wade-Driver at BRAD uses puppy personality profiles to screen assistance dog candidates, but also adds her own preferred ingredients into her selection criteria.

- Size: Because she trains many balance assistance dogs, Lydia wants to start with a large, big-boned dog. Her stud dog, a huge yellow Labrador appropriately named Sequoia, weighs more than 100 pounds and is very strong. She mainly acquires Golden Retrievers, Labs, and Lab mixes for her program.

- General health: She looks for bloodlines with a history of robust good health.

- Versatility: She wants a dog who is smart enough to train quickly, but is able to adjust to a slower pace. "Disabled partners have brains that work just fine, but they move slowly," she explains.

- Natural self-discipline: Hotheaded dogs don't make good assistance dogs. Assistance dogs must be reliably capable of self-control.

- Eliminations from the list: Herding breeds such as Border Collies, because of their very rapid movements and high degree of intensity; protection breeds, such as Rottweilers and Doberman Pinschers, because of their hardwiring for security work that might surface under stress in the form of aggressive behavior; any dog who exhibits obsessive behaviors, such as a strong tennis-ball fixation, which will compete with a partner for the dog's focus.

"I get a gut feeling on the whole package," Lydia says. She places high value on comfortable eye contact with her assistance dogs. "They have to look at me with a sweet look in their eyes."

Brian Jennings, a trainer at the Massachusetts-based National Education for Assistance Dog Services (NEADS), has experience selecting and training hearing assistance dogs. *Hearing dogs* alert their partners to unheard but important sounds in the environment, such as the telephone ringing, a car horn blaring, or the smoke alarm beeping. Brian refers to these dogs as "laptop service dogs" because they are usually smaller dogs who often sit on their partner's lap, especially when the partner uses a wheelchair.

Brian rescues dogs from local shelters and trains them to be hearing dogs. He explains what he looks for in a dog.

- Temperament testing: Weeds out dogs with aggressive tendencies, which he terms "bad default behaviors"

- Curiosity: A key ingredient, because a hearing dog must demonstrate an independent desire to investigate a sound without receiving a signal to do so from his partner

- Natural inclination to retrieve: Indicates a willingness to work in a cooperative manner with a person

- Just the right amount of voice and energy: Barks and jumps around enough to alert his hearing impaired partner but not enough to annoy or startle others

- Interested: Tries to get Brian to engage, even though he's a stranger to the dog

- Exhibits social attraction: Focuses on the environment and other people, solicits attention (soliciting attention and focusing on other people is less desirable for other types of assistance dogs, such as balance dogs, who should maintain their focus on their partners)

"Each of the trainers selects their own shelter dogs," says Brian. "Based on the trainer's own personality, some are good at building up dogs who are on the shy side and some are good at talking down dogs who are on the assertive side. It's the right match that's important."

Kali Kosch, director of training for Assistance Dogs of America in Swanton, Ohio, likes to observe prospective assistance puppies on more than one occasion. "Puppies can change," she says. If possible, she watches each puppy's interaction with her littermates for the following signs:

- Confidence, but not bullying
- Tolerance, but not whining
- Ability to recover from being startled, but not hardness or stubbornness
- Independence, but not aggression
- Gentleness when using his mouth in play, but not shyness

There are many tools available to help owners judge the suitability of a dog as their future companion. Some of them are specific tests, and others are reactions formed as a result of experience and instinct. No assistance dog training center wants to be saddled with difficult-to-train dogs or lots of program dropouts, so evaluating canine candidates is an important tool. Although predicting the future is not an exact science, the trainers have developed ways to tip the balance in their favor.

Their knowledge of the intended role of the dog and their evaluation of the traits and skills of the trainer tie the various characteristics together into a single focus. These two facets form the basis for the selection criteria for assistance dogs, and they can help companion dog owners pick a good match for their family, too.

CHOOSING CHASE

About eight years ago, when my Labrador Retrievers had attained senior status, I decided to acquire a dog of another breed. I wanted a dog who would grow to no more than thirty pounds, shed less than a Lab, get along with other dogs, and have the energy and drive to learn the sport of dog agility with me. After much research, I settled on the Border Terrier. "Border Terrier people" sent me to a breeder in the South who was an accomplished agility competitor and was planning to breed a litter of puppies. She owned both the sire and dam of the litter, and both dogs had earned many agility titles.

When the puppies were ready to go to their new homes, the breeder selected a bold, lively female for me. She is my beloved Dash, my first agility dog, now an AKC Master Agility Champion.

When Dash turned 3 years old, the breeder announced that she would be breeding the final litter from Dash's sire and dam. After this last litter, both dogs would retire from agility and from parenthood. I quickly reserved a male puppy.

When I arrived at the breeder's home to pick up my pup, she said, "Go ahead, take your pick." There were three males in the litter. "You pick for me," I responded. "You did such a good job last time picking Dash for me." "No," she smiled, "you pick your own puppy this time."

I had not come prepared with a puppy test to administer, and the breeder didn't use any formal test. I took the pups out into the yard, and they all followed me with interest, played with toys, and investigated the environment. None appeared to be too shy or too pushy.

"What are their eating habits like?" I asked.

"Well," the breeder answered, "that one puts his head down and eats his entire meal before he lifts his head up again. He's the only male who eats that way. The others take their time."

"I'll take him," I blurted out. I figured I could train a dog who showed that much interest in food!

As it turned out, Chase, now 5 years old, is a wonderful companion dog, easy to train, and a talented and titled agility competitor, but not for the reason I first thought. When he's working, he concentrates so hard that he's really not very interested in treats as rewards, so he doesn't have the love of food treats I had expected. The work itself rewards him. His eating habits actually suggested that he seriously and thoroughly applied himself to the task at hand, not that he was particularly food motivated. Of course he enjoys treats, but the chance to run an agility sequence again trumps all other considerations as a reward.

When choosing Chase, I had already taken into account important breed factors and their consequences for my lifestyle: his sex, size, grooming needs, amiability with other dogs, existence of desirable characteristics in the individual breeding line, and high energy level. I wasn't as scientific as I thought when I selected Chase based on his food motivation. However, I have capitalized on his strengths, both expected and unexpected, and he has blossomed into one of the finest dogs I have ever owned.

WHAT ROLE WILL YOUR DOG PLAY?

Assistance dog trainers know exactly what a puppy or dog placed in their program must learn to do and what type of trainers and training program the dog will experience. That model determines what characteristics they look for in a puppy or adult dog. Therefore, you have a bit of work to do before you begin to evaluate a particular puppy or dog as your future companion.

First, you need to evaluate yourself. Think about your lifestyle and probable training habits. Consider these aspects of your companion dog's future environment before you begin your search for a puppy or consider taking on an adult dog.

- Your home environment: Do you live in an apartment, townhouse, home with a yard, or on a farm? Is the orderliness and neatness of your home of particular importance to you? How often will someone be at home with the dog? Are there children or elderly family members living at home? What ages? Are there other pets in the home?

- Your intentions: Why do you want a dog? As a home companion for an elderly person, to compete in agility or obedience trials with you, to herd sheep, to join you on your cross-country skiing expeditions, to go camping with you, as a companion for your children?

- Your personality characteristics: Are you exuberant, shy, strict, soft-hearted, impatient, moody?

- Your physical characteristics: Are you strong and athletic, frail, injured, overweight, younger or older?

- Size: What dog will have the physical size required to be the companion you want?

- Grooming requirements: Do you enjoy the beauty of a lush, beautiful coat on your dog (and own a powerful vacuum cleaner), or do you require a "wash and wear" dog?

- Voice: How much barking can you handle?

- Energy level: Behavior problems result when a dog has more energy than she can discharge daily.

- Temperament: Is the best dog for you easygoing and social, independent, highly driven to work and play, attentive to only you?

Now, use your responses to develop a general picture of a dog who would suit you. Let's include three additional factors in the selection process: drive, breed hardwiring, and default behaviors.

Drives

Every dog has a combination of pack drive (interest in the family) and prey drive (interest in activities). Pack drive brings out social behaviors, such as lying next to your chair while you are reading, staying by your side on a walk, not pulling against the leash, and coming when called. Prey drive brings out working behaviors such as chasing rabbits or tennis balls, following the scent trail of an animal, digging to find prey, retrieving, pulling against a restraint, and carrying objects.

Although you want a friendly companion dog who will focus on you, you also want a dog who has enough prey drive to play vigorously. Prey drive expressed in the desire to play provides the dog with a way of relieving the stress of living in the complex and demanding environment of human society. A dog without good prey drive and playing skills will be easily frustrated, anxious, and less motivated.

Corporate executives exercise at the gym to retain their sanity, clear their heads, and stay sharp in the pressure-filled business world. Assistance dogs must be highly focused on their partners, concentrate on the business at hand, and then use their prey drive, in the form of play, to relieve the stress built up by their work. As we will see in chapter 7, assistance dog trainers teach wheelchair-bound partners how to use tug games to relax and refocus their working dogs.

A sweet puppy or dog who climbs up into your lap and stays there may tempt you, but look for a pup or dog who engages with you and then wants to explore and play, then returns to you once again.

Each dog also has some level of flight drive and fight drive. Flight drive brings out retreating behaviors such as cowering, refusing to enter the car or the vet's office, hiding from children who pester her, and running away from startling events such as hearing the car door slam or being approached by a large stranger. Fight drive brings out offensive behaviors such as becoming agitated and barking loudly in the car or the vet's office, grabbing toys from people, nipping children who pester her, barking at the car door when it slams, and attempting to make an approaching stranger back down.

You can see why assistance dogs must demonstrate a healthy balance between flight and fight drives. An assistance dog cannot retreat from scary situations, leaving her partner unattended. Nor can she aggressively attempt to control the situations to her liking. She must learn to control *herself*.

There are times when every dog will go into flight mode or fight mode. These states of mind are not exclusive in a dog. Remember that balance is the key. An overabundance of flight drive results in a painfully shy companion dog, and an overabundance of fight drive results in an unpredictably aggressive dog.

Puppy Aptitude and Temperament Testing

Many expert trainers have developed their own puppy aptitude or temperament test to use when evaluating a puppy. Here are some of the basic traits most of their tests evaluate.

Trait	Behavioral Indicators
Pack drive	Sociability, attraction to humans and other dogs, interest in being led by another dog or by a human, need to attain high social status, enjoyment of grooming and petting, comes when called
Prey drive	Playfulness, retrieving, barking, stalking, sniffing, pulling, interest in moving objects, guarding, digging, roaming
Sensitivity	Degree of influence of sound (noises), touch, and sight (unfamiliar or moving objects) stimulus; reaction to obstacles in dog's path
Flight drive	Running away, hiding, fearfulness, whining, urinating, trembling
Fight drive	Biting/nipping, growling, persistence, grabbing, hoarding, guarding
Physical soundness	Stability of movement, correct structure, good eyesight and hearing

Consider the balance of flight and fight drive in a dog who will suit your lifestyle. If you have young children and want a dog who would rather fall back in times of stress, for the safety of your children, choose a laidback pup whose flight drive tips the scales. If you want a high-energy agility competitor, like I do, choose a dog with the natural spunk to push through challenging situations assertively and continue to work with confidence.

Breed Hardwiring

On the first night of a beginner obedience training class, I always give the students this assignment: They must determine what breed or breeds are present in their dog's makeup; they must gather a bit of information about what characteristics these breeds display by talking with a breeder, consulting with their

Anticipating Breed-Specific Behaviors

The breed types listed here are just a sampling of the types of dogs bred to do these kinds of work. Many other breeds were also developed for these and other jobs.

Bred for Work	Breed Type	Some Behavioral Characteristics
Herding cattle, sheep Pulling loads Security Protection	Sheltie Border Collie Corgi German Shepherd Dog Doberman Pinscher Siberian Husky	Independent Courageous Highly focused on tasks Needs little direction Strong willed Devoted Requires lots of socialization to become a successful family pet Needs exercise and work to do
Indicating, flushing, and retrieving feathered game in the field	Pointers Retrievers Setters Spaniels	Hearty Loyal Works on direction of the handler Speedy Intelligent Amiable as a family pet Needs exercise and work to do Good companion for outdoor activities enthusiast Trustworthy Socializes gracefully

veterinarian, or reading about the breed(s) in books, magazines, or on the Internet; and they must think about how these breed characteristics will influence the training process they are about to undertake. Not only do my students learn a lot about their dog's hardwired behaviors, they actually learn to *look closely* at their dogs as a complex being.

Bred for Work	Breed Type	Some Behavioral Characteristics
Tracking game by sight or scent trail, alone or in packs	Beagle Dachshund Basset Hound Greyhound Whippet	Alerts handler by barking and baying Highly focused on and distracted by moving objects and scents Patient Single-minded Tolerant of multi-dog living environment
Hunting small game in close conditions	Fox Terrier Border Terrier Kerry Blue Terrier Scottish Terrier Miniature Schnauzer	Tenacious Loud Cunning Spunky Determined and persistent Loyal Quick Energy to spare Needs proper socialization to avoid excessive scrappiness Not especially tolerant of multi-terrier living environment
Companion; controlling nuisance vermin	Papillion Pekingese Pomeranian Toy Poodle Pug	Bright Sensitive Refined Aristocratic Amount of drive widely differs; some are not especially athletic With good socialization, will fit gracefully into a home environment and will travel well

The purposeful, controlled breeding of dogs to perform specific work has produced identifiable characteristics that become hardwired into dogs at the genetic level. That means some of the characteristics of a particular breed are passed down from generation to generation, making them generally predictable. One or two specific breed types usually dominate in mixed breed dogs.

That's not to say that picking a dog of a particular breed is like picking out a tomato from a basketful of tomatoes at the supermarket produce department. One tomato is pretty much the same as another, but dogs are a complex species and individuals differ within a breed. However, the breed makeup of a dog often tips the scales of behavior in a predictable way.

For instance, my Labradors, bred to sit quietly by a hunter's side in a duck blind, silently waiting to be sent to retrieve a shot bird, were much more successful at learning "stay" than my Border Terriers have been. Border Terriers were bred to chase fox and other vermin through the countryside, roust them from their underground dens, and expel them so a hunter could shoot them. Asking one of them to sit still in a "stay" for several minutes is like asking Old Faithful not to erupt for awhile. Good luck with that! If performing a long "stay" is part of any activity I will want to do with my terriers, I know I have a lot more training ahead of me than I did with my Labs.

My Labradors enjoyed our boating trips much more than my terriers, because they are a waterfowl breed and they loved the water so much. The Labradors were great obedience dogs, because they were focused and precise. My terriers are great agility dogs because they are quick and independent. Although some terriers excel in obedience work, and I watch Labs running agility quite nicely, prospective owners can get a glimpse of the dog's likely behavior habits and adjust their training techniques based on an assessment of breed characteristics.

Default Behaviors

Default behaviors can arise as the result of breeding or learning. Default behaviors emerge when a dog becomes so stressed or excited that she does not mentally connect with her training experiences, but behaves according to deeply seated drives or fears resulting from instinctive or learned behavior.

For instance, when one of my Border Terriers was a puppy, he was walking under the open refrigerator door when a package of cheese fell off the door and hit him on the head. He's a soft guy anyway, so of course, he became afraid of refrigerators and walking underneath objects. After working to desensitize him to the refrigerator and to objects raised in the air, he improved greatly. However, if I'm standing up and drop an object near him, he still startles more than most dogs although he recovers more quickly each time. The more I completely ignore his exaggerated startles at home when, say, I drop a book on the floor, the quicker he recovers the next time. However, I'm careful that no one standing around us near the crowded agility ring is tossing around a hard ball or toy that might come down and knock him on the head right before we run. I've adjusted my training and handling to accommodate his default behavior where it's most likely to arise and undermine our work.

If you can recognize and remember your dog's default behaviors, you will be able to anticipate situations before they arise. We already know that assistance dog trainers have developed the ability to anticipate a situation and sense the dog's likely response to it, providing the trainers with opportunities to teach rather than to react.

Here's where puppy temperament tests and adult dog personality profiles make a great contribution when selecting a dog. They help to reveal a dog's default behaviors in advance by evaluating the dog's responses to carefully constructed exercises. If you can uncover a dog's key default behaviors in advance and stay alert for any that develop later, you will get a picture of what kinds of training situations you might face in the future.

Are you, as the handler and trainer, a likely good match with the handling and training needs of your prospective pup?

TESS

Many years ago, Bill, a man about 30 years old, arrived at the first session of one of my beginner obedience classes. He brought along his 2-year-old female Siberian Husky, Tess. She was beautifully groomed and looked healthy and well fed. I could sense that he was very fond of the dog.

At the end of the first session, he approached me in utter frustration. Tess pulled incessantly on her leash. No one else could walk her except Bill, and it was all he could do to control her. She had pulled his mother down the front stairs, knocking her to the ground. Walking Tess on a harness instead of a collar just made things worse. Taking Tess anywhere was almost impossible, including to the vet. She was starting to pick up some other unwanted behaviors, too, such as digging in the yard. Bill loved the dog, but she refused to learn polite walking and she was ruining his yard. She was headed for the local animal shelter. Our class represented her last chance.

I asked Bill what he did for a living. He said he was an auto mechanic. His father had been a mechanic, and Bill had always loved cars and enjoyed working on engines since he was a kid. He now managed the very successful auto-repair garage his father had founded, and his father worked there on occasion.

I asked Bill what he liked to do in his spare time. He answered that he liked to ride his mountain bike.

"Imagine," I said, "that, because of an unfortunate family circumstance, you have to sell your auto garage and stop working as a mechanic. Not only that, but you have to sell your cars and tools, too." Bill started shifting around uncomfortably.

"OK," I continued, "now imagine that you come to live at my house for a while and I am an auto mechanic by trade. You see my cars, engines, and tools all over the place, every day, but I don't allow you to touch them. Every time you try to get near them I stop you, and even yell at you. How would you feel about that?" Bill looked very sad. "What would you do?" I asked.

"I don't know. I can't even imagine that," he answered. "I'd be a basket case without cars."

Then, I invited Bill to think about Tess. She sprang from a proud line of dogs bred for many generations to pull sleds loaded with supplies across the frozen ground of the Arctic for days at a time. It's in her blood. It drives and compels her. Donning hardware (in her case, a collar and a leash, or a harness) that actually provides her with the ability to pull against something is absolute heaven to Tess. She blossoms as she cheerfully throws her weight into the task. It feels so right.

But pulling always results in punishment and a deterioration of the relationship with her owner. Why? How can something that feels this good be so bad? Tess has no answer, but she does have a building frustration level.

When her ancestors rested after their work, they dug themselves a hollow in the snow, curled up, and slept. Tess tried to relax in the yard, but attracted more yelling from Bill for creating her deep resting places in the cool dirt under a shade tree. Sadly, Tess was becoming a basket case.

Thankfully, after our talk, Bill got to work right away. He bought an inexpensive pulling harness and set of lightweight traces (the lines used to connect a sled dog's harness with the sled). He grabbed two discarded tires from his garage and headed out to the park with Tess. He placed Tess in the harness, connected the traces, and hooked the two tires to the lines. He trotted behind the tires, holding the lines, and Tess pulled those tires all around that park for most of the afternoon. When he walked Tess back to the car, guess what? No more pulling on the leash. What a relief for both of them!

My next instruction to Bill: Repeat as necessary. The more Tess pulled the tires in the park, the less she pulled on her leash during walks. She finally could release all of that pent-up Siberian Husky drive to pull in an acceptable way.

Then Bill selected a remote, shady corner of his yard, removed the turf from a Siberian Husky–sized area, roughed up the dirt, and placed a couple of

Tess's toys on the spot. He allowed her to dig in that area only. Ahhh, finally a place to rest, Siberian Husky style!

But the best part was that Bill began to *admire* Tess's ability to pull so strongly and gracefully, a trait that had once annoyed him. He appreciated her efficient structure and smooth gait that made pulling a load effortless, and delighted in her eagerness to accept the harness. He enjoyed the sight of her contentedly resting under the tree after a visit to the park.

A few weeks after our last class, I spied Bill and Tess on the service road paralleling the road where I was driving. He had hitched Tess to the harness and traces and she was pulling Bill, who was seated on his mountain bike. Both Bill and Tess looked really happy. Later, he told me he planned to buy a set of cross-country skis and teach Tess how to pull him in the snow.

Who knows if Bill would have chosen a Siberian Husky if he had known in advance what she would require to help her become a suitable companion dog. Luckily, his love for Tess inspired him to make the effort to understand her hardwiring and satisfy her Siberian Husky needs, so she could satisfy his need for a well-behaved companion dog.

Consider the type of work a prospective dog was bred to accomplish and think about the personality and behavioral traits that might accompany the dog. Do they suit you?

Think about a puppy or dog you might want to welcome into your family to fulfill your desire for a loving canine companion. Start with an examination of the *breed* of dog and end with an examination of the *individual* dog. Are you prepared to understand and fulfill your dog's needs, based upon her breed hard-wiring in general and your knowledge of that dog in particular?

If so, your relationship will grow into your own personal mutual admiration society!

Chapter 5

Evaluating the Dog You Have

A couple of years ago, Connie Knisely, a staff trainer at the St. Francis of Assisi Service Dog Foundation, received a call from a friend who thought she might have a lead on a good hearing dog for the Foundation's program. The friend had noticed a dog hanging around and eating out of a Dumpster at a small strip mall near her home in central Virginia. She thought the dog "looked smart and friendly," and had seen him around the Dumpster for several weeks without a collar or identification tags, so she concluded he was a stray. She took the dog from the mall parking lot, fed him a good meal, and treated him for a heavy tick, flea, and burr infestation. She brought the dog to her veterinarian, who pronounced him malnourished but essentially healthy, and not yet a year old.

Over the next few weeks, Connie's friend had become impressed with the little, thirty-pound male Border Collie mix she named Tigger. He learned fast, had a stable and friendly temperament, loved treats, and now was physically fit and quite agile. She asked Connie if she was interested in him for work at St. Francis. Connie decided to check out the dog because she did have a potential partner looking for a hearing assistance dog.

"I went to meet Tigger," Connie recalls, "and found him to be a great dog. I took along some toys and a whistle and informally tested his sensitivity to sounds. He displayed good food motivation and three other essential characteristics of a good hearing assistance dog: curiosity, fleetness of foot, and a natural desire to retrieve. Also, he wasn't afraid of anything."

Stray dogs in suburban settings with naturally well-balanced temperaments receive a lot of socialization from their complex environment and can become some of the best socialized dogs in the community, showing confidence in new situations and little fear of unfamiliar things.

Hearing assistance dogs alert their hearing-impaired partners to sounds in the environment. They are trained to investigate the sound, alert their part-ner to the existence of the sound, and identify the location of the sound. Because the partner cannot hear the dog's natural alert indication, which is a bark, the hearing dog physically leaves the partner's side and goes to the source of the sound as his alert behavior. This behavior is different from the behavior of physical assistance dogs, who are required to remain within about two feet of their partner at all times. Sometimes small hearing dogs rush from their partner's lap to the source of the sound and back again several times until their partner releases them from the alert. For instance, if the doorbell rings, a hear-ing dog might jump from his partner's lap and run to the front door and back again, showing his partner that an important sound has occurred and that it's coming from the front door.

Hearing dog trainers look for different characteristics in hearing dogs than they do in physical assistance dogs. Curiosity, agility, and a desire to retrieve top the list. Connie explains, "Of course, a desire to retrieve generally indicates the dog's willingness to work in cooperation with humans. But if you think about it, we are asking a hearing assistance dog to 'retrieve' a sound. We are asking the dog to go after an interesting sound and bring it back to his partner. This act greatly resembles the physical act of retrieving an object. Dogs who want to retrieve physical objects usually can be trained to retrieve sounds, too, and enjoy it just as much."

Connie pointed out that people with hearing disabilities often have bal-ance problems, too, due to the impairment of their inner ear function. "I ask potential partners with a hearing impairment, 'Do you want a hearing assis-tance dog or a balance assistance dog? One dog can't perform both roles.'" A hearing assistance dog will be small, agile, fast, and constantly curious. A bal-ance assistance dog will be large, controlled in movement, and will wait for direction from his partner before taking any action. Connie looks for a partner who wants a hearing assistance dog more than a balance assistance dog.

Connie brought Tigger to St. Francis, where he completed his training as a hearing assistance dog. Tigger's partner is a middle-aged professional woman who works as an accountant at the headquarters of an upscale men's clothing store. She has complete hearing loss in one ear and limited hearing in the other ear. Although she has not lost her hearing completely, in her initial interview she told Connie she would feel much safer with a dog in her house and accom-panying her in public because her hearing is so limited. She and Tigger now are inseparable.

Watch Carefully

The St. Francis of Assisi trainers evaluate a dog's initial and subsequent responses to the items and events he will encounter in everyday life as an assistance dog, and they do this in a variety of settings. They observe dogs interacting with children, other dogs, wheelchairs, canes, hospital beds, crowds, riding in a car, playing, going into tight places, being petted, making eye contact, and so on. They assess the dog's physical soundness and housetraining. They check the dog's sensitivity to new sounds and sights.

For a dog I was thinking of adding to my family, I would want to observe him in the company of other dogs, among pieces of agility equipment, riding in the car, reacting to treats and toys, and displaying a willingness to follow me and then to leave me to play. I would look at the dog's physical structure and what it tells me about his ability to jump with ease.

Think about what you will ask your dog to do as your companion and observe him in these situations. If you want to take your dog to dog shows but he's afraid to ride in the car, you know what new skills he will require: riding in the car comfortably. Is he a shy dog? Then your car training will be gentle and filled with rewards. Is your dog wildly out of control in the car? Then your car training will include calming signals and rewards for good behavior choices, and each training session will be short.

Her office is on the loft level of the largest store in the chain. A carpeted staircase in the store leads up to the management offices that overlook the sales floor below. At first, Tigger remained in his partner's office, parked at the door and on alert for any important sounds. After some time, Tigger became acquainted with regular visitors to the store who were associates of the firm or who were friends of his partner. He began to recognize these "regulars" as soon as they entered the store. Today, Tigger maintains his position at the top of the staircase, just a few steps away from his partner's office door. With his head hanging over the top step, he monitors the activities in the offices and in the store at the same time. Whenever a "regular" enters the store, Tigger alerts his partner that an important person has just arrived.

Connie and her friend understood that Tigger's small size and natural behavioral characteristics lent themselves to hearing assistance work rather than to physical assistance work. They quickly recognized Tigger's strong desire to retrieve and his high energy level. Working within this combination of strengths and limitations, Connie was able to produce a wonderful hearing assistance dog and companion from an untrained, mongrel, Dumpster-diving stray dog. Tigger's impromptu socialization as a stray gave him a leg up. (The foundation's policy about accepting strays into the assistance dog program has changed since Tigger's arrival, training, and placement. Although the foundation knew and trusted Connie's friend and was certain that Tigger was a stray, it cannot be sure about the status of all dogs without owners who are found by or offered to the foundation. Therefore, to avoid inadvertently taking in a lost pet, the foundation now only evaluates dogs without owners after they have been thoroughly processed through a local animal shelter.)

Although Tigger was a stray with no formal training, Connie and her friend were able to quickly and truly *see* the dog, with all his limitations and strengths, and teach him a complex repertoire of behaviors and social skills. They weren't looking at who they wanted the dog to be; they were looking, with clear eyes and no preconceptions, at who the dog actually was, and what work they had ahead of them as trainers.

LOOKING AT YOUR DOG REALISTICALLY

So many dog owners I have encountered are tied up in frustrated thoughts about who they wish their dog could be, while the reality of the dog bears little resemblance to the owner's picture. But the owner doesn't apply the training needed to make the picture the reality. Within limits, you can socialize and train your dog to be what you would like him to be, but only if you can see what he really is today and can visualize an appropriate socialization and training path to the future.

Remember that your dog draws on breed hardwiring, his own particular levels of drive, natural and learned default behaviors, and other influences— just as your own your genetic makeup, family history, early upbringing, and natural talents influence your emotional state and behaviors. I am naturally introverted and clumsy. These are my personal limitations. No one could ever turn me into a stand-up comic or a ballet dancer, no matter how much training I received. However, with patience and good instruction from an observant instructor, I was able to learn to move smoothly around an agility course and attain my goal of participating in the sport with my dogs. I'm still not a ballet dancer, but I feel like one sometimes during an agility run!

I am not suggesting that you can change your dog from a lap dog into a field dog or from a shy dog into a party-hopper. What I am suggesting is that you observe your dog and make judgments about who he really is, including his strengths and limitations. Then, take that information and help him to become the best dog he can be. Help your shy dog develop more emotional vigor so he can accompany you to more places. Help your hard-charging socialite to learn that you will guide his behavior into more acceptable modes of interaction so that he will be welcome in more places as your companion.

Keep your goals realistic, based on your evaluation of your dog, but strive for improvements that will broaden your dog's possibilities as your companion. I know how to run an advanced agility course, but I haven't stopped taking lessons. My dogs and I will never be world-class competitors, but we will keep improving our skills. And, more important, by working together at our own level and pace, we will deepen our relationship.

A couple of months ago I was sitting under my tent at a local agility competition. (Agility competitors set up tents and sunshades around the agility rings where the dogs run the courses. They can watch the action in the rings in the comfort of their shelter and keep their dogs shaded between runs.) Another competitor sat three tents away from mine with her dog in front of her tent. She was competing with a very nice spaniel that weekend.

She was seated in a camp chair just outside her tent, chatting with a friend, with her leashed dog lying on the grass in front of her. Every time a person, or a person and dog, passed by the tent, the spaniel rushed out to the end of the leash and barked. The leash jerked hard when the spaniel reached the end and the owner scolded, "Knock it off, buster" and yanked the dog back to the front of her chair. The dog lay back down, then repeated the behavior again the next time someone walked by. I watched this occur regularly for *hours*. As time passed, the handler's tone became harsher and the yanks on the leash increased in intensity. I could tell the frustration level of the handler was skyrocketing.

I was surprised that someone who trained her dog in the complex sport of dog agility could allow this situation to escalate. But she just didn't *see* her dog, more for lack of attention than for lack of knowledge about training. I awaited the moment when the handler would simply say "stay" and "quiet" to her dog when she first noticed a passerby coming along, *in anticipation of her dog's expected behavior*, and then reward her dog for maintaining his position as directed. But that moment never happened, and the dog and handler remained at odds for the afternoon. She never applied her considerable training skills to the problem because she never fully tuned in to her dog or the situation.

I heard this handler tell her friend that her dog "just wouldn't stop that lunging behavior," although she hoped he would "grow out of it and get used to being at agility trials." Hoping does not result in behavioral modification in dogs—or in humans, for that matter. Really seeing your dog, assessing his strengths and limitations, and applying well-thought-out socialization and training where needed do result in behavioral modification. If a stray but well-socialized dog like Tigger could learn to be a highly successful companion and hearing assistance dog, then that spaniel, already accustomed to being trained by a human, could certainly learn to stop lunging at passersby.

There are few guarantees when it comes to dogs. A prospective private client once asked me if I would return his money after I coached him about training his dog if his dog did not learn all the things he wanted him to learn and behave the way he wanted him to behave. Of course I refused, just as a doctor will not cancel his bill if his treatment does not completely cure your health problem. The doctor might try another course of treatment or tell you that, realistically, although he has improved your health, he cannot heal you completely. Too many factors influence the outcome, and many are out of our control. There are limitations.

Evaluating a dog as a good candidate for assistance work does not mean the trainer now has an ironclad assurance that the dog will work out. It means the trainer has identified characteristics in the dog that most successful assistance dogs have. How it all comes together is another story. Lovely dogs wash out of assistance dog training programs, sometimes at the last minute, because they don't have the desired combination of traits and skills needed for the role. Some develop health problems.

Does this mean that the training program has no value because it doesn't guarantee that it will produce a skilled assistance dog at the end? Of course not. The washouts go on to become exceptional family dogs, drug detection dogs, search-and-rescue dogs, therapy dogs, and more.

Social skills training will not ensure that your dog will now act like a highly trained assistance dog. It ensures that your dog will develop into his best self, that his life opportunities will expand as his emotional skills improve, that your bond will grow stronger, and that you will have shaped him into the most well-adjusted and welcome dog he can be.

LOOK BEFORE YOU LEAP

Without exception, when I ask assistance and therapy dog trainers what is the first thing they do when they acquire a new pup or adult dog in their training program, they answer, "Nothing besides observe them." The trainers consider an observational period to be an up-front investment that will enable them to collect information about the particular dog for whom the trainer needs to construct an efficient training program.

Brian Jennings says he observes shelter dogs brought to NEADS as prospective hearing dogs for up to two weeks before he begins obedience or socialization training. "You have to become a trainer for *that* dog, not for all dogs," he says. And to do that, you have to know who the dog is.

He also wants to identify any default behaviors in adult dogs that will be their fallback behaviors when they are in public and are especially stressed or fearful. Unwanted default behaviors can be overlaid with more desirable behaviors as a result of training and support, but Brian must recognize and note the dog's natural fallback positions before he starts any training.

Many of the beginner obedience class instructors in my training club use simple adult dog personality profiles to help owners learn how to observe their dogs. A nationally known dog trainer, Wendy Volhard makes her Canine Personality Profile available to dog owners, trainers, and instructors on her web site, www.volhard.com/training/cpp.htm.

WHAT WE CAN LEARN FROM EVALUATING THERAPY DOGS

Therapy dog and handler team trainers know a lot about how to evaluate adult dogs and their owners. Therapy dogs are the pets of caring owners who choose to share the company of their dog with people who enjoy dogs but do not own a dog or cannot be with their dog. Therapy teams may visit nursing homes, rehabilitation institutions, hospitals, retirement centers, and even schools.

Most therapy dog owners get their dog as a pet and then embark upon the adventure of therapy dog work later in their dog's life. Therefore, most dogs who enter therapy work have not been specially selected or trained for the task in advance. But their strengths and limitations, as they apply to this kind of work, have been assessed before they complete a therapy dog program.

Not every dog and handler has the characteristics of a successful therapy team. It's important that everyone, including the handler, dog, institutional staff, and people being visited, have a satisfactory experience. No institution wants to deal with hard-to-control dogs, insensitive handlers, minor injuries to people or dogs, or any unpleasantness that could taint the reputation of therapy dog programs or the institution itself.

The Delta Society evaluates, trains, registers, and supports therapy dog and handler teams throughout the world in its Pet Partners program. Delta certifies Pet Partner evaluators, who then determine the suitability of dog and handler

VOLHARD CANINE PERSONALITY PROFILE©

Your dog's personality profile, also known as Canine Personality Profile (CPP)

To help you understand how to approach your dog's training, we developed Volhard's Personality Profile for Dogs. The Profile catalogs ten behaviors in each drive that influence the dog's responses and which are useful to us in training. The ten behaviors chosen are those that most closely represent the strengths of the dog in each of the drives. The Profile does not pretend to include all behaviors seen in a dog, nor the complexity of their interaction. Although it is an admittedly crude index of your dog's behavior, you will find it surprisingly accurate.

The results of the Profile will give you a better understanding of why your dog is the way he is and the most successful way to train him. You can then make use of his strengths, avoid needless confusion, and greatly reduce the time it takes to train him.

Evaluating the Profile

When completing the Profile, keep in mind that it was devised for a house dog or pet with an enriched environment, perhaps even a little training, and not a dog tied out in the yard or kept solely in a kennel—such dogs have fewer opportunities to express as many behaviors as a house dog. Answers should indicate those behaviors your dog would exhibit if he had not already been trained to do otherwise. For example, did he jump on people to greet them, or jump on the counter to steal food, before he was trained not to do so?

The fight part of the defense drive does not fully express itself until the dog is mature, around two to four years of age, depending on the breed, although you may see tendencies toward those behaviors earlier. Young dogs tend to exhibit more flight behaviors than older dogs.

The Questionnaire

The questionnaire for the profile suggests three possible answers to each question with a corresponding point value. The possible answers and their corresponding values are:

Almost always—10

Sometimes—5

Hardly ever—0

For example, if your dog is a Beagle, the answer to the question "When presented with the opportunity, does your dog sniff the ground or air?" is probably "Almost always," giving him a score of 10.

You may not have had the chance to observe all of these behaviors, in which case you leave the answer blank.

When presented with the opportunity:

1 Does YOUR DOG sniff the ground or air a lot?	10 5 0	Almost always Sometimes Hardly ever
2 Does YOUR DOG get along with other dogs?	10 5 0	Almost always Sometimes Hardly ever
3 Does YOUR DOG stand its ground or investigate strange objects or sounds?	10 5 0	Almost always Sometimes Hardly ever
4 Does YOUR DOG run away from new situations?	10 5 0	Almost always Sometimes Hardly ever
5 Does YOUR DOG get excited by moving objects, such as bikes or squirrels?	10 5 0	Almost always Sometimes Hardly ever
6 Does YOUR DOG get along with people?	10 5 0	Almost always Sometimes Hardly ever
7 Does YOUR DOG like to play tug of war games to win?	10 5 0	Almost always Sometimes Hardly ever
8 Does YOUR DOG hide behind you when unable to cope?	10 5 0	Almost always Sometimes Hardly ever
9 Does YOUR DOG stalk cats, other dogs or things in the grass?	10 5 0	Almost always Sometimes Hardly ever
10 Does YOUR DOG bark when left alone?	10 5 0	Almost always Sometimes Hardly ever

11 Does YOUR DOG bark or growl in a deep tone?	10	Almost always
	5	Sometimes
	0	Hardly ever
12 Does YOUR DOG act fearful in unfamiliar situations?	10	Almost always
	5	Sometimes
	0	Hardly ever
13 Does YOUR DOG, when excited, bark in a high-pitched voice?	10	Almost always
	5	Sometimes
	0	Hardly ever
14 Does YOUR DOG solicit petting or like to snuggle with you?	10	Almost always
	5	Sometimes
	0	Hardly ever
15 Does YOUR DOG guard territory?	10	Almost always
	5	Sometimes
	0	Hardly ever
16 Does YOUR DOG tremble or whine when unsure?	10	Almost always
	5	Sometimes
	0	Hardly ever
17 Does YOUR DOG pounce on toys?	10	Almost always
	5	Sometimes
	0	Hardly ever
18 Does YOUR DOG like to be groomed?	10	Almost always
	5	Sometimes
	0	Hardly ever
19 Does YOUR DOG guard food or toys?	10	Almost always
	5	Sometimes
	0	Hardly ever
20 Does YOUR DOG crawl or turn upside down when reprimanded?	10	Almost always
	5	Sometimes
	0	Hardly ever
21 Does YOUR DOG shake and "kill" toys?	10	Almost always
	5	Sometimes
	0	Hardly ever
22 Does YOUR DOG seek eye contact with you?	10	Almost always
	5	Sometimes
	0	Hardly ever
23 Does YOUR DOG dislike being petted?	10	Almost always
	5	Sometimes
	0	Hardly ever

24 Is YOUR DOG reluctant to come close to you when called?	10	Almost always
	5	Sometimes
	0	Hardly ever
25 Does YOUR DOG steal food or garbage?	10	Almost always
	5	Sometimes
	0	Hardly ever
26 Does YOUR DOG follow you around like a shadow?	10	Almost always
	5	Sometimes
	0	Hardly ever
27 Does YOUR DOG dislike being groomed or bathed?	10	Almost always
	5	Sometimes
	0	Hardly ever
28 Does YOUR DOG have difficulty standing still when groomed?	10	Almost always
	5	Sometimes
	0	Hardly ever
29 Does YOUR DOG like to carry things?	10	Almost always
	5	Sometimes
	0	Hardly ever
30 Does YOUR DOG play a lot with other dogs?	10	Almost always
	5	Sometimes
	0	Hardly ever
31 Does YOUR DOG guard the owner(s)?	10	Almost always
	5	Sometimes
	0	Hardly ever
32 Does YOUR DOG cringe when someone strange bends over him/her?	10	Almost always
	5	Sometimes
	0	Hardly ever
33 Does YOUR DOG wolf down food?	10	Almost always
	5	Sometimes
	0	Hardly ever
34 Does YOUR DOG jump up to greet people?	10	Almost always
	5	Sometimes
	0	Hardly ever
35 Does YOUR DOG like to fight with other dogs?	10	Almost always
	5	Sometimes
	0	Hardly ever
36 Does YOUR DOG urinate during greeting behavior?	10	Almost always
	5	Sometimes
	0	Hardly ever

37	Does YOUR DOG like to dig and bury things?	10	Almost always
		5	Sometimes
		0	Hardly ever
38	Does YOUR DOG show reproductive behaviors, such as courting or mounting other dogs?	10	Almost always
		5	Sometimes
		0	Hardly ever
39	Does YOUR DOG get picked on by other dogs (Either now or when it was young?)	10	Almost always
		5	Sometimes
		0	Hardly ever
40	Does YOUR DOG tend to bite when cornered?	10	Almost always
		5	Sometimes
		0	Hardly ever

Scoring the Profile

Question	1	2	3	4
	5	6	7	8
	9	10	11	12
	13	14	15	16
	17	18	19	20
	21	22	23	24
	25	26	27	28
	29	30	31	32
	33	34	35	36
	37	38	39	40
	Total Prey Drive	**Total Pack Drive**	**Total Fight Drive**	**Total Flight Drive**

teams for pet therapy work. Many institutions require pet therapy teams to obtain Delta Society certification before participating in the program at their site. When evaluating a prospective therapy dog, the Delta Society looks for the following general characteristics:

- Behaviorally reliable, predictable, and controllable
- Shows no shyness, aggression, or fear
- Demonstrates nonthreatening or neutral body posture
- Wags his tail in a friendly manner or keeps it relaxed
- Has a soft-appearing body (not tense) and a relaxed face
- Vocalizes minimally

Jan Stice, a certified Delta Society Pet Partners evaluator and member of my local dog-training club, shares another important aspect of therapy dog evaluations. "I make no differentiation between big and little dogs when I evaluate them," she says. Many owners of small dogs do therapy dog work and melt at the sight of their ten-pound cutie snuggled in the lap of an entranced, wheelchair-bound person or cuddling on the bed with a willing nursing home resident. These owners often end up applying a separate, more lenient set of behavioral standards to their small dogs, thinking that the little ones can't really injure anyone or be as disruptive as large dogs.

In her therapy team training classes, Jan maintains the same standards for big and small dogs. "Big dogs can knock people over when they jump up, but little dogs can scratch and tear the thin skin of elderly or ill patients when *they* jump up. In my classes, the first time a dog jumps up during a simulated visit, the handler corrects the behavior. The second time the dog jumps up, the team must retreat and the handler refreshes the dog's training about not jumping up, no matter if the dog weighs ten pounds or a hundred pounds."

As you assess your dog's limitations and strengths and apply the personality profiling techniques contained in this chapter, be sure not to make more indulgent judgments or accommodations based on your dog's physical size. A "sit" is a "sit" and a bite is a bite, no matter the size of the butt or the teeth.

Lest we become too focused upon asking a dog to "jump through a bunch of hoops" to qualify as our pet, let's also concentrate on developing the characteristics that qualify us to bring one of these fine animals into our family.

Therapy dog evaluators appraise the dog and handler together as a working team. While we have spent much time discussing how to evaluate a puppy or dog as your potential companion, and how to assess your adult dog's strengths and limitations, therapy dog evaluators will now have us turn some attention to ourselves in the appraisal process! Their screening process applies to both the dogs *and* the handlers.

Delta's *Pet Partners Team Training Manual* describes the general attributes required of a good therapy dog handler:

- Makes eye contact and smiles in a friendly way
- Anticipates the dog's responses and behaviors and uses cues to help the dog be successful
- Ensures the well-being of the dog at all times
- Does not use a loud voice or jerk on the dog's leash
- Demonstrates gentle interaction with the dog
- Displays confidence and a relaxed, natural state toward people and the dog
- Talks to, praises, cues, encourages, and reassures the dog throughout the visit

What would happen if your dog had the opportunity to apply this simple evaluation to *you* as a prospective handler before he agreed to become your lifelong companion? How would your dog assess your strengths and limitations as a handler based on these criteria?

This checklist doesn't require any type of complicated training skills, a scientific understanding of dog psychology, or an in-depth study of animal behavior. If you ask me, it just outlines the basic tenets of common manners and consideration for a fellow living creature, not to mention a beloved family member.

These therapy team characteristics serve as helpful reminders of the outward reflection of the relationship we aspire to with our dogs.

DASH AND CHASE

My two Border Terriers have the same sire and dam but were born three years apart. Sharpening my powers of observing and evaluating each of my dogs the way assistance and therapy dog trainers do has helped me become a much better handler.

Dash, a fifteen-pound spayed female now almost 8 years old, is bold, confident, and energetic. She loves to learn new things. Her savvy breeder selected her for me at 8 weeks old from a large litter as a "starter" agility dog. When I made the many mistakes a novice agility handler makes, such as using confusing hand signals, delivering directional cues too fast or too slowly, inadvertently cutting off my dog's running path, and basically acting like an out-of-control stick figure out on the course, Dash took it all in stride. She didn't mind doing the wrong thing (I was not good at hiding my frustration with mistakes then, so she always knew when we made an error) because she knew it was my fault! She retained her enthusiasm for the sport in spite of my ups and downs as a handler. Later, with instruction and practice, I began to approach her level of performance, finally giving her the reward she had waited for so patiently: a handler who meets her standards.

However, Dash is what a lot of dog trainers call an "impolite" dog. She adores other dogs, the bigger the better, and rushes right up to them, face to face, exuberantly saying (in canine terms), "Hi! I'm Dash. Who are you?" As we will discover in the next chapter, civilized canines consider this greeting quite impertinent, and it can be downright dangerous when the other dog has serious "personal space" issues. The trouble is, Dash and I spend fifteen to twenty weekends a year on the grounds of an agility trial with more than a hundred other dogs, in close conditions, and on high alert for the game. Knowing Dash, I have to watch her closely or she could become a light snack as she greets some big dog all charged up after an agility run. I closely monitor her interactions with unfamiliar dogs and never allow her to socialize at ringside, where tensions run highest.

Chase, a 5-year old, twenty-pound neutered male, is a great agility dog for an experienced, sensitive handler. He has wonderful drive and gives the sport his all, but making a mistake completely deflates him. If we make an error on the course, I run the rest of the course without giving him any indication that we disqualified, not even a sigh or the slightest hesitation. If I do, he will slow down and actually become physically lower to the ground, slinking through the rest of his run. He worries about being wrong.

He loves to do things well that he already knows, so he enjoys practicing agility more than Dash, who has an "I know all that already" attitude about anything approaching training drills. Actually, she's right.

Chase is one of those dogs with personal space issues and tolerates Dash's behavior at home only because she is his beloved sister and ahead of him in the pack rank. At agility trials, I look out for approaching impolite dogs and step in front of Chase to block their rush to meet him if their owner is inattentive. Chase would just rather be left alone by other dogs. He wants us to get to the work at hand. I help create an environment for him that he likes, while teaching him how to handle it better himself, to the extent of his ability.

With Dash, training sessions are short, interesting, and varied. With Chase, training sessions are rewarding and positive. Both dogs continue to astound me with their performance and love of the sport. Neither would make good therapy dogs because they have very high energy levels and Chase would not enjoy working in close quarters with other dogs.

Taking the time to understand my dogs' strengths and limitations has not required a huge additional investment of time. In fact, it has saved me a lot of time because I have used fewer ineffective training techniques, taken fewer wrong turns in the training process, and created fewer inadvertent, unwanted behaviors that require "untraining" later.

But that's not the best payback. What thrills me the most is that I have seen and felt the response of my dogs to my efforts to understand them as individuals in all aspects of our lives together. "You really know who I am!" they seem to say with their eyes, where I find reflected the confidence and security that comes with genuinely feeling understood. I am so happy to give them this simple gift. After all, they shower me with their doggie gifts every day.

Chapter 6

Communicating Across Species

After the assistance dog trainers have evaluated and selected a dog for their program, they embark on a training plan that includes socialization and behavior skills. Being efficient trainers, they want to get it right the first time. Doing so saves time, reduces the need for retraining later, establishes desirable default behaviors in the dog right from the start, and builds a better relationship with each dog by ensuring that most interactions are tailored to meet the dog's needs and have positive outcomes.

So how do the trainers determine if they are on the right training path for a particular dog? How will you determine if your training choices are working well for your dog from the beginning and when it is easier to make adjustments as needed?

As with most ongoing, complex interactions, such as a marriage, several siblings living in the same household, training an assistance dog, or training a canine family companion, good communication is the key to success. If we communicate our desires properly to a caring listener, we have the best chance of having them taken into consideration and being accommodated.

When you make plans to go shopping together with your friend, you can simply tell her you're not happy that she's always late. You both share a verbal language upon which you rely heavily to communicate. But how can you tell your dog that you're not happy that she's always late in her response to coming when you call her? Dogs rely very little on vocalizations and have no verbal language.

When you meet your friend at the mall, you sense that she and her son argued before she left her house. Although she doesn't mention it until later, you notice that her step is slightly slower, her eyes are sadder, she doesn't laugh much at your jokes, and her voice is softer and less modulated than normal. You know that she and her son are often at odds. You decide not to mention that you're annoyed about her constant lateness because you sense that she is upset today. Can you tell when your dog's emotional state suggests that you refrain from training for the moment?

Of course, other mall shoppers don't notice your friend's subtle signs of stress because they don't know your friend at all, so they don't know much about her normal step, eyes, or voice. However, if she started to cry in the store, everyone would know she was distressed because that behavior blatantly expresses trouble in humans.

If your dog holds her breath and tucks her ears back on her head when she sees your neighbor's child, only you may notice it as a sign that she dislikes the boy. But everyone will know how much she dislikes the child if your dog bites him. If you're a wise owner, you'll heed your dog's breathing and ear carriage when she's in the company of your neighbor's child and carefully monitor their interactions to avoid a confrontation. If you're an inattentive owner who has ignored your dog's cues about her feelings toward the boy, you'll soon be dealing with an unfortunate situation.

Can you just look at your dog and determine her physical and emotional state because you know her so well? Should you adjust your plan for a training session based upon what you see?

Absolutely! In her book *The Invisible Leash,* veterinarian and trainer Myrna Milani says, "Many owners . . . view *normal* training as aligning their dog's perceptual world with their own." That would be like putting me in a wig and a big dress, depositing me on the stage of the Metropolitan Opera, and asking me to perform. No matter how hard I try, there's no way I'm going to take the stage and sing opera. I would not be able to align myself with that highly defined world. I simply don't have all the necessary skills. I would look ridiculous and feel confused and embarrassed, and the audience would be highly disappointed. Ignoring indications about my state of mind and trying to forcefully align me with the world of opera would cause a frustrating failure. Pushing me onto the stage even after noting that I'm desperately trying to avoid it would not be the way to train me to perform better in the future.

Asking your dog to adjust to entirely human methods of communication will also produce disappointing results, although many dogs do try hard to accommodate us. Reading natural canine communications from your dog and offering communications that your dog can naturally understand will make communicating with your dog much more effective. It will add an otherwise unattainable efficiency and enjoyment to your training program. Assistance and therapy dog trainers rely on their knowledge of canine communications to get the job done right, without negative consequences.

THE ROLE OF STRESS

Stress represents an important part of the socialization process for assistance and therapy dogs. Some types of stress are harmful, but others, when applied properly, assist in the training process.

- Acute direct stress: Quick onset or acute stress occurs when some aspect of the dog's environment has a negative impact on the dog, overtaxing her physical systems or mental capacities. The dog's ability to take in and act on cues from her environment diminishes as she focuses only on the perceived threat. When an aggressive dog charges another dog, the victim prepares for the attack and does not hear her owner calling her away. All the dog's physical systems switch to self-defense mode. The dog's heart races and her muscles tense. Her mouth, which contains her best weapons, opens in readiness and pushes forward. This type of stress undermines communication and learning.

- Chronic stress: Some chronic stressors, such as minor pain, cause low-level reactions such as annoyance. More serious chronic stressors, such as intense pain, long-term isolation from others, and extremes in temperature, eventually interfere with a dog's overall well-being by inhibiting appetite, exacerbating allergies, and suppressing her immune system. This type of stress also undermines communication and learning.

- Short-term pressure: Low-level stress of a short, predictable duration actually benefits training and learning. Not intense enough to shut down the dog and not lengthy enough to cause declining health, this kind of pressure brings about adaptation. And the ability of any organism to adapt gracefully to environmental stresses improves its ability to survive, mature, grow, and learn. The first time an assistance dog warily approaches a man wearing a hat and discovers the man is not a threat, the dog begins to learn that men in hats do not signal danger. The more times the dog experiences this pressure to face an unfamiliar situation and habituate to it, the more experiences move from the stressor side of her internal ledger to the neutral or pleasant side of her internal ledger. Many men in hats will appear in an assistance dog's life. Her adaption to this element of her life, by undergoing the pressure to investigate it and learn its true nature as a nonthreat, provides her with information and skills that will efficiently eliminate lots of stress later in her life.

As we will see in chapter 7, assistance dog trainers carefully and deliberately place short-term environmental pressure on a dog as an important socialization tool. They read the intensity of the pressure and the dog's reaction to it by closely watching her canine communication signals. The trainers learn to read the individual communication signals *from each dog*. In return, they communicate supportive information to the dog using these same signals.

Therefore, before we undertake the assistance dog trainers' socialization program, we will learn to read the communications our dog will send us so that we can make needed adjustments to our training.

THE LANGUAGE BARRIER BECOMES THE LANGUAGE BRIDGE

As primates, humans communicate with other primates using distinct tools or codes: verbal language, body language, and even smell (perfume, natural body odors, and so on). As canids, dogs communicate with other dogs using body posture or carriage, scent, and vocalizations.

Dogs observe their owners for endless hours and eventually develop an amazing understanding of the confusing array of human vocalizations, habits of expression, and body language—many so very different from the dog's own. When humans make the same effort to read and understand canine communications, they, in turn, learn to decipher the language and expressions of their dog.

The chart on page 83 shows some of the ways in which human and canine communications are different.

Human and Canine Communication

Activity or Feeling	The Human Way	The Canine Way
Greet in a friendly way	Lean toward person Approach face to face Make eye contact Hug and kiss Shake hands	Lean backward or maintain neutral body posture Approach from the side Avoid eye contact Wait for cues about acceptable physical contact
Push someone away	Use hands	Use body, primarily shoulders and hips
Become overly excited or stressed	Speak louder, yell Gesture with hands and arms Use high-pitched tone of voice and exaggerated body language	Become quiet Become still Work to defuse the situation
Decide on direction of travel	Point with arm and hand Approach to the front of another person	Turn whole body Follow another dog and approach from behind
Caress your canine companion	Repeatedly pat top of dog's head	Long strokes on body with tongue
Training/learning	Use verbal sounds ("signals")	Watch movements of trainer (human or canine)
Primary means of communicating with same species	Verbal language	Visual cues taken from posture and carriage
Peeing and pooping	Rather disgusting	Rather interesting; it's full of compelling communications

Based on these distinctions between how humans and dogs communicate their intentions and emotions in various situations, it's a wonder we successfully coexist at all! The fact that we do coexist so well pays tribute to the ability of dogs to learn and adapt as best they can to confusing interactions with their human owners.

On the other hand, humans and dogs do share significant similarities between their species, which gives us a fighting chance of coexisting harmoniously and a basis of commonality for working out our different communication techniques.

- Dogs and humans live in social groups where status matters and the group members are well aware of the social status of each of the other members. Body language and visual cues convey social status.
- Dogs and humans play with well-matched partners into adulthood, thereby establishing play as a valuable, lifelong communication tool.
- Dogs and humans maintain a sense of personal space around themselves and around others. Their communications change when personal space is violated.
- Dogs and humans enjoy grooming activities. Physical activities that simulate grooming, such as petting, communicate pleasant feelings to others.
- Dogs and humans make long, low-pitched sounds to slow down the action and make short, high-pitched sounds to speed it up.
- Dogs and humans take short, shallow breaths when they are stressed or fearful and long, deep breaths when they are relaxed.
- Dogs and humans are highly individual, even within small subcategories such as breed or country of birth. Particular habits of communication differ among individuals. The deepest communication comes from looking at the whole picture.

Assistance dog trainers aren't satisfied with trainer and dog teams or partner and dog teams who adapt to each other "as best they can." To complete the complex training they have planned for the dogs, the trainers aspire to a much higher level of communication.

If a dog decides she wants to learn how to communicate better with humans, she could enroll in an English language class (if she was able!). If a human decides she wants to communicate better with her dog, she can learn the language of the dog, as assistance dog trainers have done.

All assistance dog trainers provide puppy raisers with detailed information about how to read visual signals from their dogs about state of mind. The trainers monitor the dog's reaction to training activities by watching carefully for these signals. It's easy to get distracted with the skills training and forget to check for subtle communications from your dog. Assistance dog trainers remind the puppy raisers to keep the lines of communication open with their dogs.

Stressed and Neutral Signals

If you learn the language of the dog, you will be able to create a socialization and training program that makes sense to your dog and in which you will have great confidence because you will be able to evaluate the process at every step. The first step is learning to understand when your dog is doing fine and when her stress level starts to intensify.

Canine Neutral and Stress Signals

Signal Type	Neutral	Stressed
Breathing	Steady, regular	Panting, shallow and rapid, puffing out lips, holding breath
Eyes	Soft, blinking normally	Whites showing, bug-eyed, dilated pupils, hard looking and staring intensely, flicking around gaze, pinpoint pupils, squinting, glazed
Mouth	Slightly open, corners relaxed	Lip licking, showing or baring teeth, chattering teeth, clenched jaw, corners pressed forward, wrinkled lips
Ears	Standing or folded in normal position	Stiffly erect, pinched, flattened to the head
Head and neck	Held in normal position, soft expression	Whipping around, wrinkled brow, turned away, extended neck, head lowered and still
Tail	Normal position, wagging widely, jauntily	Base held high, wagging stiffly or slowly or narrowly, tucked and motionless, drooping, wagging frantically, fluffed out
Paws	Loose, relaxed toes	Tight, gripping surface with toes
Stance	Balanced posture, relaxed legs, soft angles	Leaning forward, stiff-legged, highly upright posture, on tip-toes

continues

Signal Type	Neutral	Stressed
Motion	Maintains comfortable distance, can remain still	Pacing, lunging, hiding, crowding, very slow and deliberate movements, hesitation, retreating or fleeing, sniffing the ground, freezing, digging, pawing, chewing
Body	Coat laying normally, maintains housetraining, no self-directed destructive behaviors	Hackles up, turning to the side, trembling, shaking, excessive elimination, sweaty pads, heavy shedding, scratching or biting at self
Vocalizations	Silent, playful barking, moderate alert barking	Whining, barking, growling, snarling, howling, keening
Behavior	Normal reactions to handler, food, and stimuli	Inability to focus, redirecting frustration to handler, loss of appetite, overreaction, increased sensitivity to touch and sound

Calming Signals

In a book of less than fifty pages titled *On Talking Terms with Dogs: Calming Signals*, Norwegian dog trainer Turid Rugaas alerted the dog-training world to the richness of canine communications. After many years of carefully observing natural dog behaviors and collecting the data, she describes what she calls "calming signals" that dogs use to communicate subtly with one another. According to Turid, wolves and domestic dogs use these signals, involving the body, face, ears, tail, sounds, movement, and expressions, to calm themselves, to calm other dogs, and to prevent conflicts.

She notes that humans tend to communicate intensely, with loud voices and exaggerated body movements. "Dogs, that is domesticated dogs, are much more subtle in their skills and use much smaller letters, so to say," she writes. "Often the signals come in quick movements, so quick that we really need to look to see them. By experience, you can learn to see these small flashes. Other dogs see them. . . . All it takes is a little practice and knowing what to look for." She adds, "If [dogs] are awake, they talk. Just like you and me."

Most owners completely miss these subtle but highly consequential messages from their dogs. Unfortunately, many dogs have given up using their "native language" at home because it has proven to have no impact at all on the people with whom they are trying to communicate. You will not want your dog to abandon this valuable tool, so you must assure her that it works.

In her book, Turid advises dog owners about how they can recognize and use calming signals with their dogs. Assistance dog trainers understand and "speak" this canine language, and use calming signals with the assistance dogs.

Here are some of these canine calming signals and how to use them with your dog.

- Sliding the eyes to the side and looking away, turning the head away: When an upset dog barks at you, turn your eyes and head away.

- Shortening the eye; that is, softening the expression by lowering the eyelids: Assistance dog trainers want eye contact with their dogs, even though dogs consider direct eye contact threatening. The trainers consciously make their eyes softer and friendly until the dogs learn that eye contact with their handler is very desirable.

- Turning the body away: Dogs turn their side or rump to other nervous dogs. When you approach an unfamiliar or nervous dog, turn your side or back to her and wait until she comes to you.

- Holding the body in a loose curve: Relaxing the muscles that keep a dog's body loose sends a calming signal.

- Licking the nose: I notice my dogs very quickly licking their noses just before an agility run (I use other means to keep myself calm!).

- Stopping in place in a relaxed stance: Allow a dog to sniff you while you stand still as an indication of your friendly intention. When I return from training an obedience class, I stand quietly and allow my dogs to sniff my jeans as soon as I come in the door so they can understand where I have been. The scent of so many unknown dogs on my clothes excites them, but allowing them to calmly investigate these smells calms them right down.

- Moving very slowly: When I want to put a leash on my neighbor's excitable dog who has escaped from her yard again, I approach her very slowly to keep her calm.

- Sitting down or lying down: If your guests make your dog nervous, ask them to sit down. When Chase wants Dash to stop asking him to play, he lies down and turns his head away.

- Yawning: Many dogs yawn when someone hugs them because they don't enjoy being hugged, which is a primate behavior. They are asking the hugger to calm down and release them. When I want Dash to stop pestering me to play, I yawn elaborately and turn my head to the side with my chin up. She gives me a sideways look and heads for her dog bed.

- Sniffing: For a while, Dash began sniffing the ground while she was running through the weave poles at competition events. She didn't sniff the ground in practice runs. I became frustrated because it slowed her down and made her less competitive. A trainer told me that my voice became louder and my hand signals more frenzied in competition at the weave poles. She suggested that I was worried about Dash's performance and Dash could sense my nervousness. She advised me to keep myself quiet while Dash ran the poles, only encouraging Dash in a very quiet voice. It worked. Dash was trying to calm me down at the weave poles.

- Body blocking: Adult dogs separate puppies who are playing too roughly by stepping between them and separating them. When Dash and Chase's play becomes too tumultuous, I step between them instead of pushing them apart with my hands.

- Approaching in a curved path: Dogs who don't know one another often approach each other using a polite, curved path. I do the same when meeting dogs I don't know.

- Licking the face, rapidly blinking, smacking the lips, lifting a paw, stretching: These calming signals occur quickly. If you watch your dog, especially when she sees another dog in the distance or a child approaching, you may notice her signaling in this way. Dash raises her paw when I'm playing too excitedly with her.

What Happens When Humans "Speak" Canine

All this observation of your dog, learning her language, and practicing its use sounds like a lot of trouble when all you want to do is teach your dog a few simple obedience commands. Many owners aren't interested in learning to communicate with their dogs. They'd rather just use old-fashioned training techniques like leash jerks and punishment. After all, they do work, after a fashion.

And learning to communicate with your dog requires *you* to learn new things, not just teach new things to your dog. It requires you to control and manage *your* behavior as well as teach self-control skills and desired behaviors to your dog.

But without understanding and using canine language, how will you create and evaluate your training plan? Owners who attribute their dog's problem behaviors to spite, stubbornness, viciousness, or stupidity leave themselves no option other than to live with the problem behavior or get rid of the dog. You can't reverse spite, stubbornness, viciousness, or stupidity with any amount of training, so what's the point of taking your dog to a training class—or so they reason. If you believe those are the reasons your dog acts inappropriately, and you can't "read" your dog's true communications about her motivations, the relationship is doomed.

But you can address miscommunication, which is the root of most issues between owners and dogs, with training.

Myrna Milani points out, "Although we often expect quite specific responses from our dogs, we offer them the most generalized cues." For example, you might say "come," "get over here," "let's go," and "hurry up" to signal your dog to come to you. If you understand the language of dogs, you will appreciate the precise nature of their communications and signal your own cues more specifically, thereby increasing your chance of success.

Verbal and visual signals based on human methods of communication only tell your dog the state of your emotions. There is no information about what you want her to do. When you yell at your dog for not coming when you call her, you're conveying to your dog that you are angry but you are not accomplishing any desirable training (you *are* accomplishing undesirable training by discouraging your dog from coming when called). If you can't understand canine, you can't figure out how to signal your dog to come and understand why she may not want to come when you call her.

A dog naturally turns to her own instincts to decide how to respond to any given situation. If you have learned your dog's language and can communicate with her, she will develop the confidence in you to respond to situations as you direct her to respond, not as she feels like responding. That's a major requirement for assistance dogs. They must rely on their partners for direction and not make their own decisions about what to do next. But dogs don't surrender their decision-making powers to those whom they do not understand or trust.

Myrna sums up the relationship between communication and training: "The goal of training isn't training: it's mutually beneficial communication."

ASSISTANCE DOG TRAINERS TALK DOG

Lucy and Pete

At the Valley View Mall socialization session, I watched Lucy, a puppy raiser for St. Francis, work with Pete, a neutered male Golden Retriever-Poodle mix donated to the foundation at the age of 5 months. That night, the group of about six puppy raisers and dogs had gathered at the end of one of the quiet

A puppy learns to accept a greeting from a young shopper,
even though he's not fond of head pats and turns away.

Puppies socialize with one another in a quiet hallway.

hallways in the mall. One at a time, each puppy raiser walked her dog out of the hallway and through the main area of the mall, while Marilyn Wilson observed the team from a short distance.

I watched Lucy and Pete take their turn. Lucy encouraged Pete to walk along the busy corridors with her. The lights were bright, children were calling and running, strollers rumbled by. Pete walked along, interested in everything.

Pete likes to maintain his personal space, but sometimes, as a working assistance dog, Pete will be required to tolerate tight quarters. He might have to ride in a crowded elevator or lie next to his partner's chair in a small meeting room or a doctor's waiting area. Lucy decided to put a little pressure on Pete's personal space and teach him how to handle it. It's a balancing act, because she must pressure Pete just enough to teach him to accept and handle invasions into his space, but not enough to scare him.

Lucy walked closer to the shop fronts, with Pete between her and the shops. She pressured him to move closer to the glass windows, invading his personal space. Pete's mouth closed, his carriage rose higher, his eyes flicked around slightly, and his pace became a bit jerky. "Support your dog," Marilyn reminded Lucy softly. Lucy spoke to Pete in soft, low, long tones, "Goooood booooooy, Pete. Eeeeeeeeasy, eeeeeeeasy. Steady. Steady." His carriage eased

Lucy pressures Pete into a tight space at the busy mall,
but watches him closely.

Lucy rewards Pete for
handling the pressure.

down, and his mouth opened again. Lucy moved away from the shops, restoring Pete's personal space. "Good man," she told him softly. She stopped, gave him a treat, and allowed him to collect himself. He lifted his head and made eye contact with Lucy. She signaled Pete to sit, and he complied immediately. Pete handled the stress and recovered quickly, and he was not too distracted by the incident to refuse to eat or deliver a requested behavior. Lucy smiled (opening her mouth and relaxing her lips) and softened her eyes. They proceeded down the corridor.

Lucy continued to work with Pete until, a few minutes later, she turned to Marilyn. "I think he's either thirsty or tired, I'm not sure," she said. "It doesn't matter which," answered Marilyn. "Let's take him for a break." Lucy had noticed that Pete's tail started to droop, his pace slowed, his head came down, and his eyes developed a glazed look, even when she was not pressuring his personal space. She knew Pete was too tired now to learn anything more. It was time for a rest.

We returned to the quiet hallway, and Lucy gave Pete a bowl of water. He lapped it up, then walked to the back of the hallway, pressed his belly against the cool floor tiles, and rested his chin on his paws with a sigh. Good work, Pete!

Lydia and June

I accompanied Lydia Wade-Driver and Danielle Moore to a socialization session with assistance dogs in training. Lydia was working with a female yellow Lab named June. (Lydia names many of her assistance dogs in honor of partners who have received a dog from her. June is one of her past recipients, now enjoying the company of her assistance dog.)

Today, they were working inside the local large chain supermarket with the dog. Of course, Lydia and the dog have public access rights to train in the market. The employees see Lydia in the store regularly, and many look forward to her visits.

Supermarkets are tricky places to socialize and train dogs. A dog's sense of smell plays an extremely important role in the dog's exploration of a new environment. But shoppers probably would not take kindly to a dog, even an assistance dog, snuffling the pyramid of peaches or tomatoes on display in the produce department. Not many folks want to purchase fruits or vegetables that have been closely inspected by a dog's wet nose! However, most partners will require their dog to accompany them to the market regularly while they shop. Proper supermarket manners are an important part of assistance dog training.

Assistance dog trainers face a training challenge: teach the dogs to control their natural instincts and refrain from sniffing in an unfamiliar environment,

Outside the supermarket, Danielle prepares her dog for the session by allowing her to investigate the parked carts.

Lydia allows June to investigate carts in motion . . .

. . . and June receives a reward for her calm demeanor and a
compliment from a new friend.

like the market, until and unless permitted to do so. The trainers must *antici-pate* that the dog is going to sniff something in the market, because the train-er must stop the dog before she actually does sniff it. It's too late when even an inexperienced dog has pressed her nose into the floral bouquets on the floor, causing shoppers to glare their disapproval and leave in a huff. The rights of public access hang on the tenuous thread of appropriate behavior in public.

Lydia teaches the dog the signal "sniff" for when it's OK to smell some-thing. She uses the signal "don't" to stop the dog from doing something she senses the dog *is going to do in the immediate future*.

Children, shoppers, and store employees create
a great socialization experience for the dogs.

As they entered the market, June communicated her delight: Her pace became jaunty, her tail came up, her pupils widened. And her nose started to twitch. The store was full of such enticing smells! Lydia read the signs, knowing what would come next. June trotted toward an open box of grapefruit, nose leading the way. "Don't," Lydia said quietly, and took a step between June and

Mmmm! All this food looks tempting, but Danielle's dog must
ignore it. Her tongue flick shows it's not an easy task.

The dog remains calm in the presence of
many unfamiliar objects, including a
handful of balloons.

the box of fruit, communicating to June that Lydia will block her if necessary.
She applied no pressure on the leash, although she would pull June away if she
persisted; the leash is the fail-safe device.

June stopped in her tracks and turned to look at Lydia. The second June
paused in her forward motion, Lydia said, "Goooooood giiiiirl, June." They

June wants to sniff the donut display,
but Lydia cautions her with a "don't."

Lydia supports June as she remains quiet despite the noisy environment.

continued through the store, June occasionally spying something she wanted to smell and Lydia reminding her with a "don't" signal.

June began to pant and crowd Lydia, not sure why she was not allowed to investigate anything with her nose. "She's becoming stressed because she's not allowed to explore this environment," Lydia explained. June swung her head toward Lydia and opened her mouth. "Quiet," Lydia said softly. June's body language told Lydia that the dog was about to bark in frustration. No barking in the supermarket, June! The dog remained quiet.

But June's indication that she was frustrated enough to bark told Lydia that the dog's stress level had gotten too high. She walked June to the aisle filled with lawn chairs, coolers, plasticware, and small children's toys hanging on round displays. "Sniff," she said. June stuck her entire head into the toy display in pleasure. Lydia spun the display, and June sniffed each item as it rotated past her nose. She walked down the aisle politely sniffing the lawn chairs, Hula-Hoops, beach buckets, and shovels. June's eyes softened, and her neck relaxed. "Thanks, I needed that," her whole demeanor seemed to say.

"OK," said Lydia, "It's time to go." She led June toward the door and watched carefully for a sign that June wanted to sniff something forbidden on the way out. "Don't," she reminded her. June complied gracefully.

Out in the parking lot, Lydia walked June around a grassy area before she put her in the car. June sniffed the grass, trees, car tires, and anything else in

Finally, something I'm permitted to sniff!

her path. We relaxed and chatted under a tree before heading back to the training center while Lydia stroked June slowly along her flank.

"When the dog trusts that eventually I will allow her to sniff, she learns to be less stressed when I tell her 'don't'," Lydia said. "I make sure I give them plenty of opportunity to sniff on my terms. My terms become non-stressful when the dogs learn that my terms include taking their needs into consideration. But I have to watch their communications to make sure I apply the stresses properly and relieve them before it all overwhelms them. I always find something for an experienced dog to sniff deeply at least once or twice an hour. More for inexperienced dogs. If I don't recognize the stress signals from the dogs and I push them too far, seventy pounds of dog could explode in a frenzy of frustration. That would be a disaster in a public supermarket."

SPEAKING CANINE IN OBEDIENCE CLASS

On the first night of a beginner obedience class at my dog club, the owners arrive without their pets. The instructor discusses the training plan for the class, the rules of the road for owners (no slapping, hitting, or jerking on the leash; clean up after your dog; bring treats and water; and so on), and canine etiquette while in class (no mugging other dogs, for example). The instructor answers the owners' questions and asks the owners what specific topics they would like to cover in class that may not already appear on the class outline.

The second night of class could be described as barely controlled chaos. Eight to ten owners, some who have never had a dog or trained one, appear with their dogs, most having received little socialization or training. The owners are overwhelmed and the dogs are hyped up by the unfamiliar environment, new people, and unknown dogs, all of whom (owners included) are radiating their over-excited state of mind like fireworks. It's stress stew for people and dogs.

I rely on canine style communications to help establish order. I greet each handler and dog team by approaching them slowly, in a slightly curved path, leading with my side. I keep my joints loose and my head slightly tilted. I avoid eye contact with the dog. I speak slowly, in low, deep tones. I let the dog sniff my hand or jeans before attempting to touch her. If the dog seems amenable to being touched, I reach slowly for her shoulder or chest, never touching the dog on the head. If the dog lunges at me in a friendly but impolite way, I step back, turn my head, and look away while standing still. I try again until the dog extends a more polite greeting. I carry extra yummy treats and offer one to each dog and quickly discover whether the dog is too stressed to eat. If two dogs get too close to each other, I separate them by moving between them with my body.

These individual introductions take only a few moments, but provide me with a wealth of canine information. I can assess the dog by watching her reaction to being touched. If the dog never stops lunging at me when we meet or refuses to take a treat from me, I know her stress level is very high and her ability to exert any self-control is very low. However, I have communicated to the dog that I am friendly and not the source of more stress in her life. Rather, I can be the source of some calming influences. I begin our classroom experience on a positive note.

It surprises me how many dogs are startled, then delighted when they happen upon a human who possesses a rudimentary knowledge of their native language. Most seem very relieved. Imagine living alone in a foreign country for months and not speaking the native language, then finally meeting someone who speaks English.

Of course, it takes more than a couple of canine-like communications to settle a dog into an accessible mode so you can apply some gentle pressure to trigger learning and adaption. But if you use canine-style communications in the teaching process, your dog will learn on two levels: she will learn how to adapt to new environments and modify her behaviors according to your wishes (traditional socialization and obedience), and she will learn to trust you as her handler and become comfortable letting go of her own instincts and emotions when it comes to decisions about how she should act, and trusting those decisions to you. And that is part of building a deep relationship.

In the introduction to her wonderful book *The Other End of the Leash*, Pat McConnell says, "It seems to be very human not to know what we're doing with our bodies, unconscious of where our hands are or that we just tilted our head. We radiate random signals like some crazed semaphore flag, while our dogs watch in confusion, their eyes rolling around in circles like cartoon dogs." That amusing picture is the polar opposite of the communication between assistance dog trainers and their dogs. The trainers realize that human communications have a profound effect on dogs, both intended and unintended, and they recognize the value of each communication dogs send to us.

Want to develop a deeper relationship with your dog based on mutual respect and understanding? Want a willing canine companion rather than an intimidated one? Want a relationship with your dog based on clarity rather than confusion? Learn to talk the talk, canine style, like the assistance dog trainers do, and watch your dog say "thanks!"

Chapter 7

Creating a Managed, Positive-Outcome Socialization Program

"You can do all of the obedience training in the world, but if you have a dog who's afraid, you're at a loss. I'd rather have a dog who's very well socialized than very well obedience trained," says Kali Kosch, director of training for Assistance Dogs of America in Swanton, Ohio.

Assistance dog trainers have perfected an approach to canine socialization that gets the job done right. Have fun introducing your dog to the wide world of encounters he will enjoy as your companion. You will be richly rewarded with a take-anywhere comrade for life.

GETTING IT RIGHT

In the 1980s, I owned a lovely black Labrador Retriever named Stormy. A bit rangier than most Labs, she came from a combination of robust hunting lines and show-ring stock. Her temperament was softer than the Labs I had owned in the past. When I first brought Stormy home as an 8-week-old puppy, she scampered under the kitchen table and stayed there for several hours until she found her equilibrium and gained enough confidence to sally forth. All of my other Labs had immediately started to explore the house as soon as they entered it for the first time.

During this time, the dog training experts started to abandon their militaristic roots and focus on more positive training methods and the importance of socializing puppies. I was convinced of the value of exposing dogs to many situations early in life to prepare them to participate fully as companions. I decided when Stormy came to our family that I would make a serious effort to socialize her.

One evening, at twilight, I was walking Stormy in our suburban neighborhood. She had been living in our home for a few weeks and had had a chance to settle down and acclimate to the environment there. The next day was trash collection day, and the neighbors all had their oversized, green, wheeled trash bins placed at the ends of their driveways.

As we turned a corner, Stormy froze and stared at one of the trash bins. A light breeze rattled its cover. Her entire body stiffened and shifted backwards. Her ears flew back, and her eyes opened wide. She held her breath and started to back away from the bin.

"Here's my chance," I thought. "Stormy needs to habituate herself to things like jumbo trash bins scattered around the neighborhood. She needs to get over her concern and not be afraid of ordinary things in the neighborhood."

I tightened the leash so she couldn't retreat. She pulled harder and tried to turn and run. I pulled her in close and attempted to inch her nearer to the bin. I said calmly, "Come on, Stormy, it's only a trash bin. Don't be afraid. Just come on up here and check it out and you'll see it's not going to hurt you."

I drew her closer and, although she began to shiver, she loosened up a bit and stepped closer to the bin after much prodding from me. "See, it was nothing," I encouraged. She looked away from me and, as soon as I released the tension on the leash, she darted away from the bin and headed toward home with a disappointed and puzzled me at the other end of the leash.

When the weather was mild, I brought my Labs to a small lake near my home every weekend morning to enjoy a swim. Stormy had been joining us on these excursions for a couple of months, but she had never entered the water. My older Lab, Morgan, retrieved her water bumper with great enthusiasm and danced around Stormy, trying to get her to venture into the lake. Stormy would trot up to the water line, get her feet wet, and step back. I sloshed into the lake up to my knees to entice her into the water. No dice.

"This is weird," I said to my husband after a few weeks. "She's a Lab, for heaven's sake! She naturally should love to swim, especially with her buddy Morgan in the water with her. Maybe she needs a bit of encouragement." I played with Stormy at the water line for a few minutes, and then I pulled her gently but firmly into the water.

As soon as she lost touch with the lake bottom she paddled around in a flurry of splashes and immediately turned back to the shore with her eyes as big as dinner plates. She didn't come near the water line again that day or for several weeks thereafter. And, worst of all, she didn't come near *me* when we were at the lake for those same several weeks. I had lost her trust in an effort to do the right thing: socialize her to new environments and experiences. Instead of a source of support and direction, I became a source of added stress for her.

As it turned out, Stormy eventually did learn to enjoy swimming, and she became an avid water retriever, but it took a long time. After our encounter at the lake, I decided that I had made unfortunate errors in my attempts to habituate Stormy to the water. Thereafter, I left her completely alone during our visits, just encouraging her when she ventured near the water, but not touching her. After many subsequent visits, she simply followed Morgan into the lake one morning and swam with her. Soon, her natural love of the water triumphed, and she swam enthusiastically on each visit.

Stormy remained afraid of large trash bins for the rest of her life. She rarely swam as close to me in the lake as the other dogs did. I always regretted that our relationship stumbled in this way during Stormy's first year with me and that I missed golden opportunities to forge a deep bond with her based on mutual trust and understanding.

Too bad I was not acquainted with an assistance dog trainer at that time! I knew that I should socialize my dogs, and I was prepared to invest the time to do so. But I didn't know that I could do it incorrectly and make matters worse. The trainers might have helped me understand that socialization can backfire unless it's performed in a way that ensures a positive outcome for the dog.

What mistakes did I make with Stormy? Well, although I recognized her softer temperament, I didn't take it into account when I planned her socialization activities. I blundered forward as if I were working with my much more confident and resilient dog, Morgan. In fact, I didn't really plan her socialization activities at all, but rather jumped in when I thought I saw an opportunity. I didn't read and respond to her body language communications in a helpful way, but rather interpreted them as something to be overcome or cancelled out. I added to her stress and forced her to retreat, and thereby allowed her to adopt retreat as a successful coping tool—retreat made the uncomfortable thing go away. I interacted with Stormy as if she fit my general mental picture of a Lab, a mentally robust, carefree dog, and not as if she was Stormy, a softer, less adaptable Lab than most.

So much for my good intentions.

Now imagine the social skills a psychiatric assistance dog must master. In the IAADP's paper *Service Dog Tasks for Psychiatric Disabilities*, author Joan Froling details the tasks required of a dog who assists his partner in "coping with emotional overload." These assistance dogs support people who become alarmed in crowds or in public places, suffer any kind of panic attack, or lose their self-control in "intolerable situations." They distract their partners in stressful circumstances with tactile stimulation (nudge or nuzzle the partner, place their head on the partner's lap, lick the partner's hand or face, paw at the partner). They recognize when a partner is having nightmares, hallucinations, or even suicidal thoughts and respond to signals to bring the TV remote or open a door or window to let in normal sounds, fresh air, and distracting stimuli. Their stated purpose is to "empower the human partner to recover and sustain emotional control in settings where uncontrolled [human] emotional reactions are unacceptable." This description means the dog must do a *better* job than his human partner of handling some stressful situations!

I didn't do a very good job of helping Stormy maintain her demeanor and gain control over her fearful emotions in a stressful situation, and I was the *human* training the dog. And yet, psychiatric assistance dogs perform this sophisticated work in support of their human partners. When the human partners can't keep it together at a particular moment, the dog must buttress his partner's efforts to regain self-control by exhibiting a ton of it himself. In the company of an obviously distressed handler, the dog must retain his focus and bolster his partner's recovery.

Yes, the assistance dog trainers had a lot to teach me about how to properly socialize a dog.

WHAT SOCIALIZATION IS

Some trainers refer to socializing dogs as "inoculating" them against future behavior problems. In other words, as a result of proper socialization, your dog will build up an "immunity" to the stress brought on by traveling to unfamiliar places, meeting all kinds of people and animals, and encountering unfamiliar objects. Building that immunity is exactly what assistance dog trainers do for assistance dogs, and it's exactly what you can do for your companion dog.

Socialization is the process of habituating a dog to a variety of things through repeated exposure. It includes teaching your dog the social skills to act appropriately in a variety of settings and with a variety of inanimate objects, animals, and people. Thus, the four targets of a comprehensive canine social-ization program are the SOAPs: settings, objects, animals, and people. Each of these target categories carries equal weight and importance.

A socialization program, as designed by assistance dog trainers, develops your dog's ability to switch his focus back and forth, from you to elements of his environment and back to you, at your direction. Your dog learns to con-centrate on you, even in highly distracting settings, and to continue to assess his environment while you are calling for his attention. It prevents distracting elements of his environment from completely usurping his consciousness.

If you want to identify your dog's default behaviors, observe him carefully during his socialization sessions. In these sessions, you will apply carefully con-structed pressure on your dog and teach him how to handle it with decorum. Note his initial or instinctive reactions to these pressures. Note his tipping point, where mere concern becomes fearfulness or aggression. Stormy's default behaviors included fear of unfamiliar environments, noise sensitivity, and the desire to flee. In planning future socialization activities, I could have antici-pated these reactions and planned how to address them in a positive way. Earlier in her life, I could have taught her alternative coping strategies and established them as healthy default behaviors. At least I did remain aware that, in times of significant stress, she might exhibit her natural, underlying default behaviors.

A socialization program complements the training of specific behaviors by preventing elements in your dog's environment from corrupting your dog's abil-ity to learn and present behaviors when you ask for them. Distractions no longer threaten your well-socialized dog's concentration, the socialization sup-ports the behavior.

According to Suzanne Clothier, socialization "builds a reference library in the dog's head." The dog experiences many new situations in a positive way and files them away in his brain under the heading "familiar, non-threatening, fully capable of being dealt with, a normal part of life, nothing to be concerned about, I've seen it already." The more situations the dog can file away in this mental category of unintimidating things, the less stress your dog will experi-ence and the more self-control he will exhibit in his life.

The good news is that the process becomes easier and faster as you work the program. Remember, efficiency ranks high on the list of desirable char-acteristics of an assistance dog training program. The trainers strive to get the job done with a reasonable amount of effort expended or to find a bet-ter way.

WHAT SOCIALIZATION ISN'T

The managed socialization of a companion dog is *not* a free-for-all. You're not going to throw your charge into stressful situations and expect him to sink or swim on his own (sorry Stormy, pun intended). Only by ensuring positive outcomes in the socialization process will you avoid having your work backfire and produce a fearful dog who suffers from problems caused by unpleasant training experiences.

The program does *not* use flooding—a term from behaviorism that describes the process of overwhelming your dog with a fearful stimulus until his fear peaks and subsides and he becomes numb to the stimulus. Proper socialization teaches your dog strategies to cope with and recover from uneasy situations rather than surrender to them.

Socialization is *not* a substitute for behavior or obedience training. Social skills represent only a portion of the well-rounded education of your dog— although they are certainly an important portion. Don't think it's enough to have a dog who is polite and comfortable in many settings but who is unable to perform specific behaviors, like "down," or "come," or "give." You must be able to direct your dog's behavior as well as count on his good manners and concentration.

Socialization is *not* a one-time event in your dog's life. It can't be accomplished in an eight-week training program and then shelved for the rest of his life. "Use it or lose it" applies here. Assistance dogs report to work and encounter the unexpected every day, which continually polishes their socialization skills until they shine. Although you may not be working the socialization program to its fullest extent all the time, you will always be looking for opportunities to keep your dog tuned up and highly socialized.

Positive-outcome socialization is *not* an accidental occurrence. Just letting your dog hang out with you a lot doesn't provide adequate socialization. Neither does letting your dog run loose with other neighborhood dogs or letting the kids manage him. It takes an adult with a good plan to socialize a dog.

Socialization is *not* an adjunct activity to running a few errands or doing a little shopping. It's an activity unto itself that requires (and deserves) your full attention. Socialization requires not only a reasonable amount of time, but also a reasonable amount of planning and management. It would be counterproductive to create your plan and then not follow through carefully at the time of the actual socialization activity.

Socialization is *not* a matter of managing your dog's feelings or reactions. It's a matter of creating and supporting your dog's coping and recovery strategies. Your dog's reactions are normal for him, no matter what they are. Ultimately, you will help him apply some self-discipline to the behaviors he offers as a result of his feelings and reactions.

Socialization is absolutely necessary, but it's *not* difficult and easily becomes a habit. Socialization can be achieved the way you eat an elephant: one small bite at a time.

Ann Hogg, a trainer at St. Francis of Assisi, suggests, "Manners first, then obedience follows." Elizabeth Broyles, also of St. Francis, agrees that socialization makes the dog "mentally ready for obedience training and develops his confidence in himself as well as in you."

Socialization *is* the single most important investment you can make in your relationship with your dog.

It Works with People, Too

The first night I attended a puppy raiser training session at St. Francis, Marilyn Wilson introduced me, told the puppy raisers that I would be observing the class regularly, and briefly explained my book project. She invited them to interact with me as they wished but said they were not required to do so.

On the first night of class, most of the puppy raisers watched me carefully. A couple of them approached me, shook my hand, smiled, and introduced themselves to me. A couple were curious about the details of my project. Several seemed stiff and wary of me and kept their distance all night, regarding me with brief sidelong glances. Some became quiet whenever I walked near them and didn't say a single word directly to me.

At the second class, several puppy raisers greeted me right away. Others acted as if they never saw me before but agreed to let me take pictures of them when I asked. One requested a business card as identification, which I presented.

On the third night, nearly everyone greeted me with smiles and by name. Several puppy raisers asked how the pictures were turning out and a couple of them offered to talk with me individually. They all brought their dogs to me to pet before class started.

By the next visit, my presence was hardly noticed, and everyone answered my questions freely.

Gradually, eventually, and each at their own speed, I watched the puppy raisers get socialized to me.

THE RULE OF SEVEN

Some dog breeders who are especially concerned about understanding puppy socialization and producing well-socialized pups for their clients have developed an interest in what has come to be known as *The Rule of Seven*. The theory finds its roots in a 1956 essay, published by psychologist George A. Miller in *Psychological Review*, titled "The Magical Number Seven, Plus or Minus Two: Some Limits on Our Capacity for Processing Information."

Miller had become interested in the many places the number seven cropped up in the world: the Seven Wonders of the World, the Seven Seas, seven primary colors, seven days in a week, and so on. He found that marketers believed people generally will not act on a piece of advertising or a television commercial until they have seen it at least six or seven times. In constructing the current system of assigning telephone numbers, he suspected that the phone company chose a seven-digit number because seven had been determined to be the maximum number of simple pieces of information a human brain could remember in the short term. He wondered what significance the number seven might have for mammalian psychology.

As a result of tests he performed on humans, Miller suggested that mammals can remember only seven unrelated items of new, simple data at a time. He called this restriction "channel capacity" or the size of the "funnel" through which unrelated facts can be processed by a mammal's brain before "overload" occurs and the accuracy of the brain's processing function declines. He saw improved accuracy of brain processing up to the seventh item, and then saw a decline.

Dog breeders and trainers have seized on this hypothesis and applied it to their obedience and socialization programs for puppies and adult dogs, each according to their own interpretation of the theory. Many breeders insist that puppies must experience each new situation seven times, but not more. Some ensure that each puppy meets seven new dogs and seven new people and visits seven new environments each week until they place the pups in their new homes on the seventh day of their seventh week. Some obedience trainers require their students to practice particular obedience exercises with their dogs six or seven times during each home training session to achieve maximum retention, but no more than seven times to avoid deterioration of the learning.

For me, the relevancy of Miller's ideas to canine socialization is the evidence that some sort of channel capacity exists in the brains of mammals, including dogs. The brain remains effective in processing simple, immediate data until certain limits are reached, and then it begins to decline in function. Seven items or repetitions might be a good estimate of this capacity.

Although we don't need to become too dogmatic about the number seven, we do need to understand that humans and dogs can only deal with so much information without going into overload. We want to work our socialization program regularly but not so intensely that it overwhelms our dog's ability to assimilate the training.

Keep in mind that your dog has a natural limit to his ability to process the experiences you will provide for him during the socialization program. Also remember that the effectiveness of repeating a learning exercise fades after a short while. It's an innate property of your dog's mammalian brain, as it is of yours. Watch for his body language communications about when his comfortable processing limits have been reached and honor these limits by not pushing him to process more than he can handle at any one time. Remember when a socialization session does not go smoothly that he is not stubborn or excessively wimpy or unusually difficult. Make sure you did not overload him with more than he could handle. Your dog has a mammalian brain, which has its natural limitations. Take them into account in your socialization plan.

FEAR PERIODS

Another popular aspect of dog training and socialization is the concept of canine fear periods, or particular times in a pup's life when he may be uniquely susceptible to long-term problems caused by harsh handling and traumatic or painful experiences. Canine behaviorists have identified the period from 8 to 10 weeks old as a critical puppy fear period, when otherwise resilient puppies who normally might bounce back from a negative experience find themselves deeply disturbed by it. At this age, wild canids emerge from their comfy dens and, under their mother's guidance, learn what aspects of the world they should fear and avoid in order to survive in the wild. Therefore, trainers believe this period offers an excellent opportunity to teach a dog what *not* to fear in his life by habituating him to his environment.

Canine behaviorists now believe that an additional fear period occurs at about 12 months of age, during a dog's adolescence. I believe Stormy lived in a low-level fear period during her early years that ebbed and flowed but didn't dissipate until adulthood, when she remained cautious but became much steadier. Morgan breezed through her fear periods without a backward glance.

Of course, owners must weigh the value of early socialization with the health risk of taking a young puppy into public places before he has received his complete vaccination protocol. Owners can mitigate the hazard by choosing low-risk environments in which to socialize their pups, but it's a controversial issue among dog trainers, owners, and veterinarians.

Some trainers focus their socialization activities in these fear periods to prevent the establishment of lifelong anxieties in the dog. They concentrate on obedience training during the more stable periods in the dog's early development. The assistance dog trainers remain alert to these periods of hypersensitivity in the dog's maturation process, but they socialize the dogs throughout all of their developmental stages and even into adulthood. The assistance dog trainers regard social exposure as the foundation for all other training activities and do not limit it to certain periods in a young dog's life.

CANINE GENERALIZATION

I have heard many dog owners ask their obedience-class instructor why their dog would respond to "sit" perfectly in their living room but would not sit in obedience class or in the backyard or when visiting at Aunt Sarah's house. "Dogs are very poor at generalizing things," is the inevitable answer. "You must show your dog that he must respond to your signal to sit in lots of places by taking him to lots of places and practicing 'sit.' He cannot generalize that your 'sit' signal, when given in the living room, means he should sit in all of these other places, too."

This concept always puzzled me. When Dash was a puppy, we regularly visited the home of my friend who owned five Bearded Collies. Dash, weighing only about eight or nine pounds, would run happily in the yard with all except the intact female of the group. The dogs were very careful of her, although they sent her tumbling once in a while. Now, even at 8 years old, Dash still becomes gleefully excited when she spies a big, hairy dog—especially if he *is* a Bearded Collie, but even if he isn't. And she hasn't seen my friend's dogs in more than six years. Isn't that reaction the result of generalization?

When we travel to attend an agility event, I don't have any trouble convincing Dash and Chase that it's dinnertime, although I am offering their food in a motel room and not in our kitchen. The first time a young child pulled Dash's ear was the last time she approached a child, *any child*, without caution. But she shows no hesitation in greeting adult humans. And, thankfully, Dash and Chase will run agility with me in an indoor arena, in an outdoor shaded ring, on grass, on sand, in the bright sunlight, on an A-frame with slats, on an A-frame without slats, in the rain, and pretty much under any conditions, even if we haven't trained for that condition specifically. These behaviors all look like canine generalizations to me.

Recently, I attended a seminar presented by Suzanne Clothier, one of my favorite canine behaviorists. In her lecture, she said dogs do generalize about things *that are important to them*. That's when it all made sense to me. When they begin their training, most dogs don't see learning to sit on cue in the living room and in the yard as really important to them. We make it important to them as time goes on by treating it as important to us. We devote considerable time and attention to it. We surround it with rewards and praise to raise its level of importance to the dog. We become animated in training sessions. Training sessions signal the arrival of interesting inter-actions and lots of fun. Soon the dog attaches meaning to this rather bland activity because of the significance we give it. That's when the dog begins to generalize his skills.

Assistance dog trainers address generalization in their training programs. Interestingly enough, for them it's both a goal and a potential problem.

The trainers teach the assistance dog that when his partner gives the signal "help," the dog must run to someone and bark or lightly bump the person to attract their attention, and then bring them to the partner who requires help. Usually, the dog practices this exercise at home with his puppy raiser and a family member. However, the trainers must teach the dog to generalize this signal. One puppy raiser explained to me, "I brought my daughter to our training class with me to show my instructor how well I taught the dog to perform 'help.' I told the dog 'help.' There were lots of people standing around, but my dog was frantically looking for my daughter because we had practiced this exercise only with her. If this had been a real situation anyone could have helped, but he ignored all of the others while searching for my daughter. He thought 'help' meant to go and get my daugh-ter. I have to work on generalizing this signal so that he asks for help from the closest available person."

The puppy raiser will help the dog generalize by starting again from the beginning with only two people. Once the handler teaches the puppy to alert to the closest of only two people, she can work the pup with three, four, and then five people, eventually asking lots of people to treat and praise her puppy for responding to requests for help, making it highly valuable to the dog to find help fast from anyone nearby. Once the pup grasps the concept of alert-ing to the *nearest* person, increasing the group to, say, ten to eleven people, will be a breeze.

You will find that the first time you introduce your dog to a rambunctious toddler in your backyard, you will have to invest some time in the process. But your dog will ace his interaction with the fifth or sixth toddler he meets, even at the park.

For assistance dogs, though, canine generalization can undermine their work. An assistance dog may be trained to alert to oncoming seizures in a child. The dog senses the onset of a seizure and alerts the child's parent to the situation by barking or pawing at the parent. However, if the child experiences seizures often, the dog might come to consider the onset of seizures as an ordinary or natural part of everyday life for the child. The dog's alert behavior might deteriorate because he has become habituated to the child's seizures and has filed them as "normal" in his mental reference library. The parents must continue to reinforce the importance of swift alert behaviors. They will then prevent generalization from developing into familiarization and then acceptance of their child's condition, and keep the dog's alert performance sharp.

For your purposes, use your dog's ability to generalize situations to create a very large inventory of normal and familiar situations in his reference library. He will learn to accept them calmly and with the proper demeanor. Remember that you are working against his natural defense mechanisms that want to file most new things as "alarming and possibly harmful" to keep him on the alert for possible life-threatening situations. Gradually teach him to re-file these things as "normal" and control his fearful behaviors, which, while appropriate in the wild, are not appropriate in human society.

When you undertake your socialization program, you will expose your dog to many situations and experiences. In the beginning, the work may seem repetitive. But you will teach your dog that it is important work to you and to him. When your dog discovers the deep meaning of these interactions with you, he will value and generalize the learning. Your socialization program will progress to a new level of efficiency, requiring less time and energy from both of you while continuing to produce sterling results.

THE SOAPS

You will expose your dog to many settings, objects, animals, and people (SOAPs) in your socialization program. Brian Jennings begins the NEADS socialization program with easy SOAPs and progresses to more difficult ones later on. Also, he identifies SOAPs that are unique to the lifestyle the dog will live as an assistance dog. The chart on page 113 shows some examples.

SOAPs for an Assistance Dog

	Easy	Difficult	Unique
Settings	Quiet places such as a bank, library, post office, a mall in the morning, the park, the dog's neighborhood, the owner's car, a quiet friend's house, stairs, the basement	Noisy, crowded places such as a supermarket, coffee shop, veterinarian's office, pet-supply shop, a mall on Saturday afternoon, elevator, noisy friend's house, a friend's car, the park during a softball game	Escalator, movie theater, human medical office, workplace or business office, hospital, bus, hair salon, restaurant
Objects	Household appliances, garbage cans, large storage box, toys, crate, grooming equipment, lawn chairs, ironing board	Bicycle, skateboard, large trash cans, boat, lawn mower, metal folding chairs, giant stuffed animals, statues, umbrellas	Wheelchair, cane, reach extender, walker, super-market cart, cash and credit cards, hairbrush, TV remote control, telephone handset, harness
Animals	Friendly dog in the partner's home, cat or other friendly pet in the partner's home	Unfriendly dog in the partner's home; friendly neighbor's dog; dogs met in pet supply shop, in the park, and at dog training class	Ducks, squirrels, cats, birds, deer, horses
People	Partner's immediate family and close friends	People unlike the partner, wearing strong perfume, large hat, heavy coat, talking loudly, smoking, running, clowns	Human healthcare professionals, taxi driver

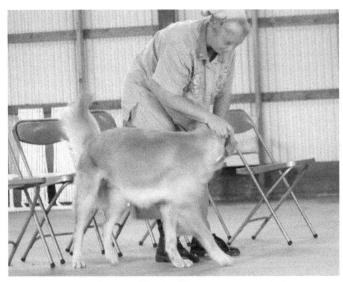

Puppy raisers acclimate the pups to negotiating
between rows of folding chairs . . .

. . . in tight spaces . . .

. . . in tight corners . . .

. . . and next to clanking grocery carts.

An assistance dog will support his partner in the movie theater, in the workplace, at a child's birthday party, and in the doctor's office. However, most companion dogs will not visit these places or meet their owners' doctors. Most companion dogs will not handle a TV remote control or a credit card. However, my companion dogs will travel to agility competitions with me, something assistance dogs will not do. The chart on page 116 shows some SOAPs for my own companion dogs.

SOAPs for My Companion Dogs

	Easy	Difficult	Unique
Settings	My home, quiet places like a bank, library, post office, the parking lot of a mall in the morning, the park, my dog's neighborhood, my dog van, a quiet friend's house, stairs	Noisy, crowded places like a supermarket parking lot, outdoor coffee shop, veterinarian's office, pet supply shop, a mall parking lot on Saturday afternoon, elevator, noisy friend's house, a friend's car, the park during a softball game	Motel room, indoor and outdoor agility trial sites, agility class sites, obedience class building, the lake, automatic doors
Objects	Household appliances, garbage cans, large storage box, toys, crate, grooming equipment, lawn chairs, ironing board, gardening tools, plastic leaf bags	Bicycle, large trash cans, boat, lawn mower, metal folding chairs, my squeaky garden cart, fireworks, strollers, hair dryer, sidewalk grates	Agility obstacles and training equipment
Animals	My other dogs, my friend's friendly dogs	My friend's neutral or unfriendly dogs, dogs in the pet supply shop, horses at farm sites where agility trials are held	Dogs belonging to other agility competitors, dogs hyped up at an agility trial
People	My husband and friends, dog-friendly neighbors	My family (all living in other states), neighbors who are not friendly to dogs, children, our veterinarian, skateboarders	Excited handlers at agility trials, agility trial judges in the ring

My dogs do not have public access rights, so they will have to stay in the parking lots of some places where assistance dogs can visit, such as food stores and restaurants. Still, we own a boat and a squeaky garden cart, live on a lake, and often enter a motel through automatic doors and ride an elevator to a room, and those pose their own challenges.

Create a table that identifies the SOAPs for your dog. Think about all the settings, objects, animals, and people your dog must habituate to as your companion. Think about all the things you will want your dog to place on the

A puppy in training tries to calm an exuberant puppy with a raised paw . . .

. . . and the puppy complies.

"familiar" side of his mental ledger, so he will respond to them with confidence and without fear or concern. Think of all the everyday and unique situations in which you will ask your dog to act with decorum and good manners.

If you own a Siberian Husky and plan to race him, add a racing sled and traces to your SOAPs list. If your dog will tour the country with you in your RV, add your RV, a variety of campsites, camping equipment, and dogs owned by other campers to your list. If you practice with a rock band in your basement, add loud music to your list. If all the kids in the neighborhood play at your house, add groups of loud children to your list. If your elderly mother visits regularly, sometimes with her friends, add seniors to your list.

Now, it's time to take our socialization program out of the planning stages and put it into action.

EARLY SOCIALIZATION

The assistance dog programs that breed their own litters let the puppies' mother begin the socialization process. Early on, when a litter of puppies she bred first became mobile, Lydia Wade-Driver noticed that the dam encouraged the pups to follow her. The dam lead them through the kennel room and out into the yard. She watched them as they explored the environment under their mother's supervision. When a puppy showed fear, the dam stopped and approached the offending object or area. Her presence calmed the pup, and she quietly waited for the pup to regain his composure and rejoin the group. She did not push any puppy to explore beyond his own inclination, nor was she overprotective or anxious.

At first, eager to socialize puppies at the first opportunity, Lydia would take the newly mobile pups and introduce them to a variety of simple situations herself. But she found that when the dam had access to the pups, she skillfully proceeded to undertake her own program of socializing them.

Lydia set up an enclosed puppy play yard adjacent to her backyard. In it she placed safe toys and objects, such as plastic blocks, rubber mats, dog toys, safe children's toys that rattle or squeak, a sheet of tough plastic, balls, pieces of rope, empty cardboard boxes, and the like. She watched the litter's dam monitor the puppies as they explored the area.

In addition, the dam refereed the puppies as they learned to interact with each other. The puppies jumped on each other, snarled and nipped, raced and played, and then snuggled together for a group nap. The dam warned puppy bullies to moderate their behavior and intercepted nipping and grabbing before any puppy was hurt.

Lydia decided that the dam accomplished socialization so successfully during the first couple of weeks of puppy mobility that Lydia returned primary responsibility for this very early socialization to her.

Lydia and her part-time assistant at BRAD, Danielle Moore, observe each puppy during this period and note the variations that begin to appear in their personalities. "Even very young puppies have likes and dislikes," says Danielle. "I watch them as they pick out a favorite toy or food on their own. I will honor these preferences later in the pup's life. If a pup loves chicken and likes to chew on a piece of rope, I will use chicken treats and provide chew materials for that pup later."

She continues, "I watch to see what each pup likes to do, what they want to learn, and what they show interest in. If a puppy offers a behavior, like picking up something and carrying it around, I will work first on picking up and carrying behaviors [an important assistance dog skill] with that dog during their behavior skills training, because I know they will enjoy the training and excel right away. I place at least three safe toys in the pup's kennel and watch which ones each puppy likes best. It keeps them busy and indicates to me which toys will motivate the pup later. Imagine how frustrating it would be to have personal likes and dislikes but live your life with little or no access to them. It's a stress I can remove from their lives."

During this time, Lydia and Danielle "swaddle" the pups, holding them close and gently touching them all over to accustom them to loving human touch. "Mainly, I hold them under my chin, next to my face. It's the main remedial action we provide to the pups," says Lydia. She swaddles the new pups when they become frightened or concerned past their ability to cope. This first lesson establishes the owner as the source of good things in the pups' lives; the pups learn that human interaction overcomes unpleasant situations. Later, a more mature pup will learn to handle difficult situations himself with support from his trainer or partner.

"Treat them like a human baby," Lydia suggests. "At this point we offer nothing traumatic, we talk to them often, even though they can't understand our verbal communications yet, and we let them sleep in a crate next to the bed. They know they can count on us."

The Breeder's Head Start

One Sunday afternoon before Stormy was born, I visited Stormy's breeder, Martha. I joined her as she released a litter of 5-week-old Labrador puppies out into the yard for a romp. All the pups shot into the yard, but the gate bounced back on its hinges before the last pup made it through, pinching the pup between the gate and the post. The pup squealed, jumped back, and the gate swung shut, trapping the pup alone outside the play area. The pup cried loudly. Before I could assimilate what had happened, Martha flew back through the gate, picked up the puppy, and pressed him to her neck. In just a few seconds the pup quieted. Martha placed him on the ground in the yard, and he cheerfully leaped ahead to rejoin the group. "Courage later, comfort now," I remember Martha saying to me.

If you purchase your pup from a breeder, ask her about the early and beginner socialization activities she performs with her puppies. Puppies who receive little attention from humans or never leave their kennel environment before being placed with an owner will lack the head start that knowledgeable breeders provide for their puppies. It's work only the dam and the breeder can do for the puppy. Ask the breeder to share with you their observations about your pup's likes, dislikes, and reactions to early life experiences.

As each puppy matures, Lydia and Danielle take a more active role in setting forth a managed, positive-outcome socialization program in preparation for the pups' release to an off-site puppy raiser. Now that you have taken your puppy or new dog into your home, you will replace the dam and the breeder as your dog's teacher, mentor, and greatest supporter.

BEGINNING SOCIALIZATION AT HOME

"I lie down on the floor with him daily to assure him that I can see things his way," says one St. Francis of Assisi puppy raiser.

In his first weeks in your home, your dog will experience many new situations, whether you are with him or not. Because you want to manage his socialization activities and ensure positive outcomes, keep your puppy with you so you can observe his reactions and manage his environment. Use baby gates to restrict his movement or snap a leash to his collar and attach it to your belt. Called the "umbilical cord" method by some trainers, your dog soon learns to travel with you throughout the house and you will have your hands free and your dog close by for observation.

Visit each room of your house with your dog and let him explore them and their contents. Note his body language for signs of fear, stress, or fatigue as he investigates each area.

Remember these guidelines during this beginning phase of socialization training.

- Work first on easy SOAPs at home.
- Do not begin puppy obedience training until after the end of the beginning socialization training.
- If your dog already knows some obedience cues, such as "sit," do not ask for them during the beginning socialization sessions.
- Do not scold or correct your pup during this socialization training with "no," "bad dog," or leash jerks (which should not be used at any time). You are habituating him to new things, gauging his reactions, and providing him with information about proper responses. His reactions can't be wrong; they are just his honest natural reactions.
- Do discourage occasional aggressive responses that follow fearful reactions by using mild verbal corrections, such as a quick and firm "uh-uh," and praise when the aggression ceases and the puppy calms down.
- Work for three to five minutes at a time.
- Work two or three times a day.
- Work this part of the program at home for about two to three weeks.
- Make sure the entire family understands the program you have planned and works in concert with it, not against it.
- Begin with the easiest SOAPs and add more difficult ones later.
- Plan a session and start it by observing your pup. Then adjust your plan according to your observations and anticipate your dog's reactions and your future training responses.
- Use treats and praise as rewards.
- Do not coddle or use baby talk with your pup during a fearful response or during an attempted retreat. Your dog will confuse your communication with praise for his inappropriate actions. Speak to him gently in a normal tone of voice and use praising verbal communications only when his decorum returns.

Let's look at an example of a beginning socialization session at home with several different puppies representing different possible reactions.

You have your puppy or new dog with you in the kitchen. You turn on the dishwasher at the other end of the room and watch your pup's reaction. He stops his motion, leans back on his legs with stiff joints, but does not run away. He presses his ears back against his head and drops his tail. You know his state of mind by reading his body communications: he has become cautious and concerned but not panicked. Speak to him softly and encourage him to relax and come slightly closer to the dishwasher.

Our first pup regains his composure and complies by walking up to the dishwasher and touching it with his nose. You reward him enthusiastically with praise and treats, then back away from the dishwasher and give him a moment to think about this interaction. Mission accomplished for now.

Our second pup remains still but is very reluctant to approach the dishwasher. You encourage him to move *just one step closer*. If he complies, reward him enthusiastically and end the session. During the next session, ask him to approach two or three steps closer.

Our third pup panics at the very thought of moving closer to the dishwasher and tries to flee the kitchen. *Do not allow him to leave and do not end the training session.* Calmly keep him in the kitchen and speak to him in a normal tone of voice until his ears come up, his breathing becomes regular, and his joints relax. When he has regained his composure, ask him to join you at the other end of the kitchen—where he stood when the dishwasher first started to run. When he returns to his original position without attempting to leave the scene and his body language indicates a more relaxed state of mind, give him a treat for holding his ground and end the session for now.

Our fourth pup shows fear and then attacks the dishwasher by barking or growling at it. *Do not remove him from the scene.* Make a soft verbal correction (such as "uh-uh") and provide a distraction, such as calling him to you or clapping your hands. Reward him the second he ceases the behavior.

Each puppy has begun to learn that whatever his *reactions* to unfamiliar or stressful situations may be, what really counts is his ability to *recover* his composure and *behave appropriately* thereafter (according to *your* definition of "appropriate").

In addition, the first pup learned that confident, well-mannered responses earn rewards.

The second pup learned that even a small step in the right direction earns a reward and his owner will not push him past small steps unless his owner believes he can handle it.

The third pup learned that panic and retreat are not acceptable options for responding to stress, but regaining and maintaining composure earn rewards.

He learned that his owner will support him but will not accept out-of-control responses.

The fourth pup learned that aggression does not make fearful things disappear from his life, but good behavior earns rewards.

All the pups learned that their owner understands them and is sensitive to their state of mind. Their owner will not ask them for more than they can deliver. Trainers refer to this technique as working "sub-threshold," meaning that you always keep the training challenging but not so stressful that it pushes the dog into panic or shut-down mode. The pups learn that self-discipline pays off and that they are capable of gracefully handling pressure from their environment.

Of course, the pups did not learn these complex lessons after just one session. But they did begin the learning and have started out on the right track. And each session ended with a positive outcome.

What would have happened if you had forced the third puppy to come close to the dishwasher immediately? His lessons would have included: the dishwasher is even scarier close up; my owner is a threat to my safety; I must learn to run faster next time; I hate the kitchen; it's best to enter new rooms with great caution because they may contain a scary dishwasher; I should react based on what I feel right away or I won't get the chance later. These lessons add stress to your dog's life and teach him nothing about how to handle that stress in a healthy way.

The next day you decide to continue the socialization training and up the ante. What will you plan for the next session?

You decide to introduce the first pup to the vacuum cleaner. It not only makes a loud noise, but it moves around, too. You bring out the vacuum cleaner and let the puppy inspect it before you turn it on. You move the pup away from the appliance and push the start button. If he reacts by showing signs of concern but he holds his ground, praise him. If, with encouragement, he approaches the running vacuum cleaner and inspects it, reward him handsomely. Many treats and much praise should follow his decision to explore with confidence.

On the second day of your program, the second and third pups are not ready for an introduction to the vacuum cleaner. The second pup, who approached the dishwasher one step closer, should work toward an even closer approach to it. The third pup, who attempted to flee the kitchen in panic, should work on holding his ground near the dishwasher and then gaining one step closer.

The fourth pup should receive rewards for eliminating aggressive behavior toward the dishwasher before moving on to the vacuum cleaner. When vacuum cleaner day arrives for him, be aware that your pup may attack first as his default behavior; be ready to distract him and reward good behavior.

If you own a puppy like the first pup, don't be tempted to think that your pup is naturally well-adjusted and therefore requires little socialization. You want your dog to exhibit signs of stress in new situations so he can learn how to handle it. It will be your job to find a reasonable and responsible way to make that happen. He must learn the valuable lessons of socialization. Brian Jennings says, "If a dog in our program seems to be so confident that he does not need these lessons, he will not make a good assistance dog." Why not? Because eventually the dog will encounter a challenging situation while he's in service and he will not have learned the skills necessary to cope with it.

Be sure your pup encounters as many different SOAPs at home as possible.

- Settings: How does he respond to changes in surfaces, from carpet to hard flooring to grass to concrete? How does he respond to darkness, to noises, to smells in each room? Does he take the stairs willingly?
- Objects: Does the big, black recycling bin scare him? How about the pile of laundry on the floor or that bag of golf clubs leaning in the corner of the mud room? What are his reactions to noisy objects (the dishwasher) and noisy objects that move (the vacuum cleaner or the garage door)?
- Animals: How does your pup react to other pets in your house or to the well-mannered pets that your friend might bring to your home?
- People: Note the pup's reaction and response to easy (you know what I mean) women, men, and children. What happens when grandma visits?

Visitors

The arrival of visitors to your home represents a great opportunity for socialization training with your pup. The training does add an extra layer of complication to a visit, and it's tempting to shut your pup in the bedroom or put him out in the yard "just this one time" so you can enjoy the visit without any worries. Resist the temptation. Not only will you fail to train your pup to show appropriate, desirable social behaviors, but you will exacerbate unwanted behaviors such as charging or scratching at the bedroom door or howling in the yard. The arrival of company will eventually signal that a highly unpleasant event is about to befall your dog—namely, social isolation. For a pack animal like a canine, social isolation is mentally very painful and frustrating.

Patiently wait for your dog to calm down in the presence of your company, even though it requires added work on your part. Praise and reward him generously when he does. Your visitors will probably find your actions interesting rather than distracting, and it's a critical part of the socialization process.

Approach an assistance dog and you will experience the calm, straightforward gaze of a confident animal, even though he has never met you. That response originates from social skills training, not from social isolation.

Other Dogs

You can do a wonderful job of socializing your dog in many settings, with objects, with people, and with pets who are not dogs, but it takes other dogs to socialize your dog to canines. Asking a human to socialize a dog to other dogs is the equivalent of asking me to teach another person Spanish language and customs. I studied Spanish for four years in school and visited Spain. I still retain a rudimentary knowledge of the language and can understand a bit of what's said to me slowly in Spanish. But I definitely do not have the skills or credentials to teach the language and customs to another person.

With observation and practice, you can read your dog's communications and "speak" his language back to him in a way that deepens your relationship. But *fluency in canine can only be taught by other skilled and fluent canines*. That's why you will select nice puppies and well-mannered, self-disciplined, socially skilled dogs to interact with your dog during the socialization process. They alone can provide the healthy canine interactions your dog requires.

Lydia starts dog-on-dog training with 8-week-old puppies held on a loose leash. She brings *one* of her adult, experienced, neutered, gentle dogs off leash and into the room with *one* puppy. The dogs interact, and Lydia praises the puppy for proper behavior and for refocusing on her when she calls the pup's name. When this interaction becomes easy (the pup's body language tells Lydia that he's confident and comfortable in the company of the adult dog), she brings two of her responsible adult dogs into the room with the puppy. When all goes well, she removes the puppy's leash and lets them all play for a short time. She carefully monitors the interaction and repeats it often. She continues to expand and change the mix by using different combinations of dogs, but all of them are chosen because Lydia knows they will interact safely with a puppy.

My Border Terrier, Chase, joined our family at an inopportune time, but he was available from a breeding that would not be repeated, and I really wanted a puppy from that litter. We lived in rural North Carolina, with few well-socialized dogs nearby and no dog clubs or puppy classes in the area (bummer!).

A Kerry Blue Terrier puppy meets an adult Golden Retriever . . .

. . . and uses a play bow to invite the Golden to interact.
The Golden stays cool . . .

. . . but when the Kerry Blue grabs his leash,
the Golden says "enough!"

An Irish Wolfhound lowers himself to the ground
to interact with this West Highland White Terrier,
whose bold nature is apparent.

Our house was on the market, so we were always tidying up and leaving on a moment's notice so a realtor could show it. Very disruptive and time-consuming.

At 6 months old, Chase began to travel with me and Dash to agility trials, but handlers at trials don't want their dogs distracted by puppies, and their dogs are usually in high gear and not in the best frame of mind to tutor a sensitive puppy anyway. I counted on Dash to carry the burden of socializing Chase to other dogs during the first year of his life. That was my mistake.

Chase never became fluent in canine. He and Dash enjoy a wonderful relationship, and they have developed lots of shortcuts in their communications. Often, I have to look closely to catch their postures and subtle visual communications because they happen so quickly and efficiently. However, Chase is not skilled in communicating with or reading unfamiliar dogs. He has not gained fluency with his body language, so he's unsure about how to signal other dogs that he's a friendly guy but protective of his personal space. He's not sure how to read the signals of approaching dogs about their intentions, so he assumes the worst (as a wild animal would normally do as a safety precaution). He becomes anxious.

A young female Labrador visits our neighbor two houses away most weekends in the summer. Her owner brings her out to swim in the lake. She's very good about staying in my neighbor's unfenced yard. Sometimes she runs around with the two Shelties who live in an adjacent house. But one day she decided to approach our fence and check out the dogs—my dogs—who live inside it. Chase and Dash were out in the yard near my husband, who was chatting over the fence with our next-door neighbor.

Chase immediately froze, compressed his body, and stared through the fence. (Dash's tail started to wag, and she started to wiggle.) The Labrador approached slowly, joints all loose, tail wagging. She curved her body and turned her head away to the side while approaching our fence slowly. (Some trainers refer to these canine signals as "cutoff signals." Turid Rugaas would call them calming signals. The Lab was trying to calm down Chase.) Chase ran to the fence on stiff legs and displayed his weapons (teeth) for her information, but holstered them again without making any noise or other aggressive moves.

My husband (good doggie dad that he is) intervened by reminding Chase to get a grip. He praised him when he could see Chase relax a bit. The Lab came up to the fence, and my neighbor petted her. Chase, his pupils still large but his breathing more regular, remained tight. The Lab lay down on the ground, then turned over, stuck her muzzle up to the fence, and licked out her tongue through the slats. Chase relaxed and lay down. He also turned onto his side and licked through the fence at the Lab. Both dogs regained their feet, shook off, and that was that.

The Labrador was highly skilled in both delivering and reading canine communications. If Dash had been in the yard without Chase, the Lab probably would have leaped right over our picket fence and joined Dash for a romp. But she knew better after reading Chase's signals. However, rather than taking him on aggressively or making matters worse, she defused the situation gracefully. That's the kind of dog you want.

We must manage Chase's interactions with other dogs, especially the initial ones, because he lacks expert canine social skills. If the visiting dog had been a grumpy intact male Chow Chow, the outcome might have been very different and we could have had a fence fight on our hands.

I strive to improve Chase's skills by conducting managed socialization exercises with him. He has improved a great deal, especially when I am at his side to support him. But I welcome future visits from the Lab. She's skilled and safe and can teach Chase a few lessons that I can't.

When I visit St. Francis, the administration building is always full of loose dogs: puppies and their puppy raisers, older program dogs in training, and the trainers' personal pets from home. Connie's Chinese Crested (weighing about fifteen pounds) walks around among the gang of big dogs as if she owns the place! The foundation maintains a waiting list of prospective owners who would like to adopt a program dog whom the trainers feel would succeed better as a pet than as an assistance dog. I know why these dogs are in such demand: They have already received "black belt" canine socialization training.

ADVANCED SOCIALIZATION ON THE ROAD

"Doing it right is much more important than doing it a lot," says Brian Jennings of NEADS. After a few weeks of beginning socialization at home, it's time to evaluate your dog's progress. When you're sure he has aced the training at home, it's time to take the program on the road. The guidelines for beginning socialization sessions still apply, with these modifications.

- Start simple beginner obedience training at home in conjunction with advanced socialization training. Practice "sit" and "down" and a few fun tricks like waving a paw. In the beginning socialization sessions, you did not require your pup to offer obedience behaviors during the sessions, but you will do so in the advanced socialization sessions.

- Complete at least twelve advanced socialization sessions before asking your dog to deliver obedience behaviors in a session.

- Work on soft eye contact and focusing your dog's attention on you at home (more about these behaviors in chapter 8). Always train in a place where you can see your dog's face and make eye contact.

- Be available when your dog makes eye contact with you. Your dog will learn that making eye contact with you will provide him with support and reassurance, especially in times of stress or uncertainty. When he turns to you, be there for him.

- Work on play tugging with your dog at home (more about this tool in chapter 8).

- Identify a safety zone wherever you train. You will not be training at home, where your dog is comfortable. So be sure to find a quiet area where you can take your dog if he becomes overly frightened or stressed or fatigued during an advanced session. Think about the St. Francis pups training at the mall: The teams returned to the secluded hallway when a dog needed a break or after a long session in the crowded main corridors. Don't bring your inexperienced dog to a church service, where you will be reluctant to leave and disrupt the service even if he needs a break.

- Work two to four times a week.

- Work no more than about thirty minutes to one hour at first, and not more than about two hours with experienced, mature dogs. Make these judgments based on your dog's behaviors and state-of-mind signals.

- Avoid repeating patterns. Mix it up. Choose a variety of difficult SOAPs.

- Remember, when you bring your dog to an outdoor café, you're there primarily to train, not to eat a meal. When you bring him to the park, you're there primarily to train, not to visit with friends.

- Watch your dog like a hawk! Marilyn Wilson says, "Training is always taking place, whether it's the training you want or something the dogs have thought of themselves. Always know what your dog is doing."

- Be on the alert for SOAPs that move. Moving objects are more difficult for dogs to habituate to than stationary ones.

- Always work sub-threshold for your dog.

This Kerry Blue Terrier pup earns a treat for negotiating a wobble board . . .

. . . and the open end of an agility chute obstacle.

I joined an advanced socialization session with Karen Hough and Jane, the Standard Poodle, at PetSmart. Earlier in the week, Karen had taken Jane into Best Buy, Target, and Staples for training. Jane had performed beautifully and offered all the obedience behaviors Karen asked for in the stores, despite the many noises, unfamiliar people, and unusual objects. However, in PetSmart, with unfamiliar dogs nearby, Jane had become stressed and would not pick up an object on the floor when Karen asked her to. Karen planned to work on this behavior because Jane needs to pick up dropped objects for her partner, Robbie.

Karen adjusts Jane's balance harness . . .

. . . and walks her in the parking lot to
allow her to collect herself.

They head for their training session inside PetSmart.
(That's me on the right taking notes.)

As Jane enters the store, Karen watches her body language closely.

"It's time for Jane to take responsibility for her actions," commented Karen. "She's advancing from following directions about appropriate responses to knowing on her own what to do in many stressful situations, but she still needs to learn how to handle the presence of strange dogs." At first, Karen calmly walked Jane around the store. Jane appeared quite relaxed but stiffened ever so slightly when an unfamiliar dog walked by her. Karen placed a comb on the floor and asked Jane to pick it up. Jane did not comply.

Jane has no problem maintaining her focus in the presence of unfamiliar people and objects . . .

. . . but is too distracted to pick up objects at Karen's request.

"Let's back up to where she's comfortable," said Karen. We moved to a quiet aisle, and Karen told Jane to sit and stay. She moved slightly away from the dog. Jane complied quickly, and a couple of calm dogs walked by without incident. "Sit" was within Jane's comfort zone. Karen praised her and then signaled Jane to down and stay. Jane complied, but her ears started to fly around on her head. She swung her head from side to side and kept her legs bunched under her body. "Down is harder," explained Karen, "especially if she expects that a strange dog may walk by at any time. It's a vulnerable position."

Karen leaves Jane in a "stand" but stays close by.

Karen moves farther away, leaving Jane in a "sit"
but watching her closely.

Now Jane must maintain her "down" in Karen's presence . . .

. . . and alone . . .

. . . and in the presence of other shoppers . . .

. . . and she does!

A dog passed by in a perpendicular aisle, and Jane popped up into a stand-ing position. "I could verbally correct her for breaking her 'down' position," said Karen. "But her stress level is high, and a correction added to it now would just put her over the edge. That undermines training and is not a positive out-come." Karen merely repositioned Jane in a "down" without comment. This time, Jane leaned over on one hip and visibly relaxed on the floor. She didn't move again, even when a dog passed by. Karen dispensed several tasty treats and heartfelt praise. She asked Jane to stand up, then walked her around for a while to be sure she was composed. She returned to the quiet aisle and placed the comb on the floor. "Pick up," Karen said quietly. Jane did so. Extra yummy treats and praise followed, to Jane's delight.

"That's enough for today," said Karen. "I'll come back another time and ask her to pick up an object in the busy part of the store. For today, she has made progress and done a great job."

Jane picks up the comb in spite of the distractions in PetSmart.

Jane makes a new friend on the way
back to the car.

We left the store, and Karen allowed Jane to sniff around the parking lot, take a drink of water, and relieve herself before returning to the car.

After a couple of additional sessions, Karen was able to place pick-up objects right under the dog toy displays in the store's busy aisle and Jane retrieved them.

Your dog needs your support when he's out in public more than anywhere else. "Do you like to sing in the shower?" asks Suzanne Clothier. "Of course you do. Well, how would you feel if your friend asked you to sing in front of her guests at a dinner party?" Generally, people don't like to be conspicuous, to be the object of attention and scrutiny from strangers. Neither does your dog, or any animal, for that matter. In the wild, it pays to blend in and can be dangerous to stand out. Also, traveling outside their own territory or home is a cause for concern for animals, because they have become more vulnerable and must monitor the unfamiliar environment as well as new objects and animals. When your dog is out in public, you can help him to conquer these natural reactions and respond to public settings with self-control and good manners. Only exposure and habituation under the guidance of a kind and patient handler produces these skills. Avoiding uncomfortable situations, especially in public, inevitably backfires; the dog develops fearful and antisocial behaviors, and you have no way to correct them.

Evaluating Each Session

The assistance dog trainers evaluate each socialization session and the dog's overall progress, and adjust their plan accordingly. Lydia asks each of her puppy raisers to complete an Outing Record each time they take a dog on a public socialization visit. Here are the questions they answer.

- Where did you go?
- What did you and the puppy do?
- What means of transportation did you use and how did the puppy behave during the trip?
- Approximately how much time did you and the puppy spend doing this activity?
- Did the puppy see anything new or unusual and how did he react?
- What did the puppy hear and how did he react?
- What kinds of surfaces did the puppy walk on and how did he react?

- Describe any problems you and the puppy encountered.
- What good experiences did you and the puppy have?
- Did any unusual situations arise with the puppy?
- Did the puppy have any problem toileting in a new place?
- How would you describe the puppy's behavior with regard to listening and responding to you?
- Describe any situations in which the puppy seemed nervous, aggressive, fearful, or resistant.
- Were there any specific behavior signals you worked on?
- Would you want to do this or a similar outing with the puppy in the future?
- Would you recommend this outing to other puppy raisers?

Kali Kosch of Assistance Dogs of America regularly asks her puppy raisers, "How much do you think you can reasonably expect from the dog at this level? Are your requests fair? Were you constantly preventing your dog from 'doing the wrong thing' or were you showing him the right thing to do? Are you tempted to be over-cautious or do you trust your dog's resilience and willingness?"

Brian Jennings cautions, "Lassie was a pretend thing. Remember, your dog is just a dog. Plan the work, break the training down into pieces the dog can grasp, return to the basics when you need to, and you will get the work done."

Jan Stice kept her eye on the therapy dog training class taking place in our dog club building while talking with me one evening. Her co-instructor, Jeanie Calhoun, was teaching handlers how to support their dogs while visiting in a nursing home or hospital environment. "Support your dog" and "Be your dog's advocate" are Jan's constant mantras in her therapy dog classes.

Jeanie, role-playing an elderly nursing home resident, was lying in a hospital bed in the center of the training room. In previous classes, each dog had approached Jeanie in the bed and learned how to lie down politely on top of the bed covers if invited to do so by the resident. But tonight, Jeanie is upping the ante and getting rough with the approaching dogs, as elderly patients will sometimes do inadvertently.

A handler approached with a Golden Retriever on leash. Jeanie started to pet the dog roughly, grabbed his collar and pulled hard, loudly stating, "I want him up here on the bed with me!" The handler asked Jeanie to release her dog and said, "Please don't pull him up. Let me get my dog up there for you." "Good work in supporting your dog," exclaimed Jan.

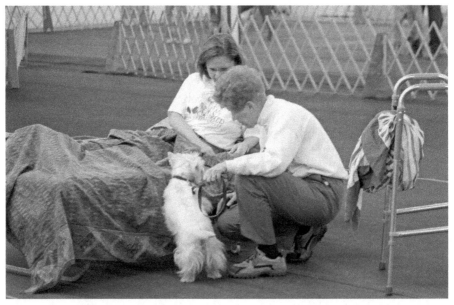

A handler brings her terrier to greet Jeanie in a hospital bed.

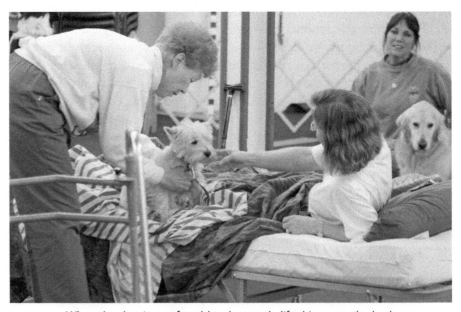

When the dog is comfortable, she gently lifts him onto the bed.

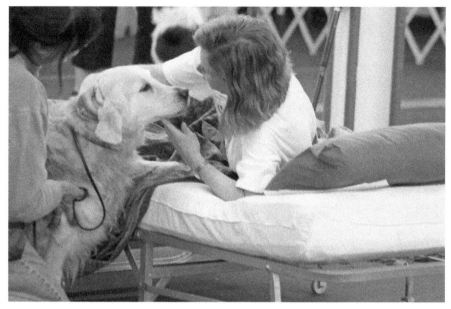

Jeanie greets a Golden Retriever . . .

. . . then tests the waters: Will he accept head pats?
Notice the big eyes and tongue flick.

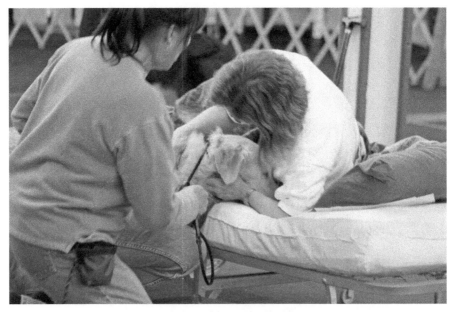

And how about big hugs?

A pup learns about wheelchairs.

A dog looks to his owner for support when confronted with a walker. . .

. . . and checks in while maintaining a "down."

A Border Collie meets a person who is
using a cane and receives a reward for
his good behavior.

A Lab mix asks his handler for help when the trainer presses for
his attention . . .

. . . and receives it.

Now, on to the challenges of walkers.

This Rhodesian Ridgeback learns to accept touches from Jeanie with decorum.

A wheelchair doesn't stop this Golden Retriever from accepting a tummy rub.

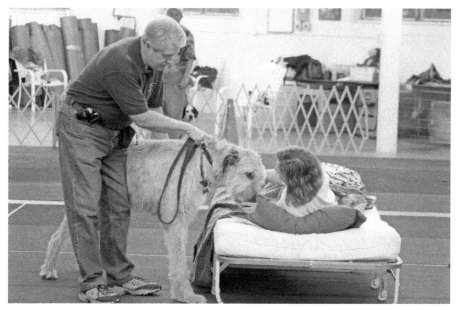

Jeanie grabs this Irish Wolfhound by the collar, but he remains composed.

Break time in therapy dog class.

"When you are out in public with your dog, supporting him is the most important thing," Jan said. "Small dogs will get grabbed and picked up, big dogs will get petted by being pounded on the head. People will lean over them in a way that threatens many dogs. Therapy dog handlers try hard to please the residents they are visiting and sometimes forget to support their dogs, who may be getting stressed. The handlers think, 'Just let me do a little bit more for everyone here today.' It's hard to leave a facility and say you're finished for the day when people look forward so much to your visits. The handlers don't want to disappoint anyone. But we teach handlers to observe their dogs and stop the training or the visiting before the dog loses his social skills due to a bad experience."

"Does the socialization training ever cease?" I asked Jan. "Well," she answered, "one of my students and her experienced Collie were visiting a nursing home recently. It happened to be a day when a resident was celebrating her birthday, and everyone was in the common room enjoying a slice of cake. The handler and her dog entered the room to greet the residents. Each of the residents had a shiny 'Happy Birthday' balloon tethered to the arm of their chair. The balloons were floating around at the ends of their lines. The Collie had seen a lot of things, but it was his first time for balloons. The dog took one look inside the room and bolted for the door in a panic. The handler couldn't do much training at the site, so she went home and tied balloons to her refrigerator door, to the bed posts, to the stair railings, and to the doorknobs, one at a time, little by little. Then she tied them outdoors to her fence posts, the car door handles, and the mailbox. She rewarded her dog for approaching the balloons until the dog cheerfully ran up to a balloon to get a treat. She went back to the facility with her dog and brought a bouquet of balloons for the residents.

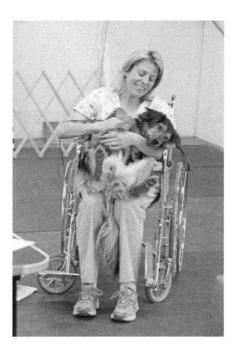

That was the end of the balloon issue for the dog. I tell my students that the moral of this story is, 'Never brush off your hands and say my dog's socialization training is done. There's always a balloon around the corner.'"

ADULT DOG-ON-DOG SOCIALIZATION

Owners with undersocialized adult dogs should take great care with dog-on-dog socialization activities. Undersocialized dogs lack the communication skills to reliably declare their intentions to other canines and to accurately read missives from unfamiliar dogs. Canine misunderstandings can easily lead to canine arguments (just as they can with humans), and somebody could get hurt.

I would never place Chase in a group of unfamiliar dogs in his current state of dog-on-dog socialization, especially because he projects his concerns outwardly rather than internalize them. He's liable to take offense or indicate a threat when none was intended. If he encounters another dog who is as unskilled at diffusing perceived threats as he is, a problem could arise.

While holding Chase on a loose leash, I carefully monitor Chase's approach to another dog, also held on a loose leash by someone I know and trust. When Chase gains his composure, I allow him to approach the dog,

Steps for Managed, Positive-Outcome Socialization

We can capture the essence of the canine socialization program by remembering these steps:
1. Develop a socialization plan.
2. Reward good behavior from the start.
3. Push the limit.
4. Read the dog's body language.
5. Re-establish composure and confidence. Do not retreat.
6. Return to the situation.
7. Reward improvements.
8. End on a positive note.
9. Evaluate the session and plan for the future.

count "one, two, three," and then walk him a short distance away. Not much misunderstanding or escalation can occur in three seconds. We use this technique in my club's beginner obedience classes, especially in the first class when the dogs are all trying to inspect each other and no one knows anything yet about the quality of the social skills of each individual dog.

When I am at an agility trial, I take Chase on walks, on leash, with my friends and their dogs. Dogs who are walking in parallel with other dogs, rather than face off with them, relax and retain their composure much better. Putting dogs in motion drains a lot of negative energy from a social encounter and redirects it to a positive activity.

If I wanted to greatly improve Chase's dog-on-dog social skills, I would enlist the aid of an experienced applied animal behaviorist who specialized in adult dog-on-dog socialization and aggression. Many of these behaviorists bring their own dogs to client meetings. These dogs have assisted their owners with many types of clients and dogs and have become expert in their ability to read canine signals and diffuse anxiety and fearfulness in other dogs. These dogs are highly skilled in their interactions with unskilled dogs, and their owners are highly skilled in managing the situation for the safety and comfort of all parties.

IT'S ONLY NATURAL

Are companion dogs really so very impressionable and prone to developing problem behaviors? Do owners of big, hearty pups with friendly, happy temperaments really need to do all this socialization training? The pet dogs owned by previous generations received little or no formal education, but most turned out all right—at least, our grandparents say they did. Sometimes it's unclear to dog owners why we have so much work on our plates these days when a puppy or dog joins our lives.

Let's reflect back on the "good old days" of pet dog ownership. I don't want my dog to be killed by a car like my aunt's unsupervised dog did one night during a family dinner. I don't want to have to hold my dog off with a broom until I can get his dinner bowl down on the floor like my neighbor, fearing a bite, did with her family pet every night. I don't want to give my dog a tranquilizer for a simple trip to our veterinarian, like my friend's family did with their dog. I don't want my dog to steal my grandmother's new leather gloves, take them under the couch, shred them, and then bite my dad when he tried to retrieve them, like my own "nice" dog did on Christmas day when I was a child.

I do want my dogs to do many things these dogs from the past never dreamed of doing: travel, stay in motels, participate in exciting canine sports, attend classes, play nicely with other dogs, enjoy the company of our guests when they visit, go to dog shows, and lots more.

Our understanding of canine psychology and behavior has grown exponentially in recent years and has provided us with ways to prevent unwanted behaviors and carefully instill desired ones. In discussing human and animal psychology in her book *Animals in Translation*, Temple Grandin describes some of this new knowledge and how we as dog owners can use it. "If you think about it, animals are constantly confronting the unknown. . . . So I think a good way to try to get inside an animals' head, to the extent that's even possible, is to be constantly asking yourself, 'How would I feel if what I were looking at right now was something I'd never laid eyes on before in my life?'"

She continues, "It's kind of horrifying to think that our survival depends on *remembering* all the bad stuff we're supposed to be afraid of. Evolution solved that problem by making fear learning *permanent*. All intensely emotional learning is permanent. That's why you can forget everything you ever learned in trigonometry, but no one born before 1958 is ever going to forget where they were when Kennedy was shot."

Animals live in a narrowly defined space between fear and familiar. Grandin says, "If you're too cautious to explore things, you miss out on things you need. Being too cautious might make you miss signs of danger, too."

In other words, if something bad happens during an exploration, animals think the exploration caused the bad thing to happen. They don't believe in coincidences, they believe in causes. They develop permanent fear memories and aversive reactions to what they believe caused the bad thing. They develop "superstitions." That's why a dog will not happily jump into a car if the only time he rides in the car is when he goes to the vet. Even if he's going to visit grandma this time. That's why a dog who has been jumped by another dog at the start line in agility will refuse to take the start line again, even when the dog who jumped him is not on the premises.

Our contemporary knowledge about how animals perceive the world and build their repertoire of behaviors in response to it provides the foundation for canine socialization. Socialization, in turn, supports the expanded role companion dogs play in modern life. Let's take advantage of it.

Chapter 8

Creating a Relationship-Based Behavior and Skills Training Program

Just before a person receives their assistance dog, they spend two to three weeks at the training center learning how to support the training the dog already has and how to teach new behaviors. They work with an assistance dog trainer and their new assistance dog every day. The recipient soon becomes adept at using contemporary, positive canine training techniques. "Disabled handlers are smart, they just don't move as fast as people without a physical or psychological impairment," says Lydia Wade-Driver. The dog they take home will continue her education under their tutelage.

Because of their disabilities, recipients can't administer leash jerk corrections, smack the dog, physically manipulate the dog's position by pulling her around by her collar or leash, restrain the dog from running off, push the dog into a "sit" or "down" position, or even yell loudly at the dog. (All of these techniques are no longer part of today's more enlightened canine training methods, but are still used by some trainers and handlers.) The recipients become masters of positive, reward-based training methods that build a strong relationship between them and their dog. The *power* of the partner arises from the deep relationship they have cultivated with the dog, and not from their ability to physically force the dog to do something. The assistance dog responds reliably to the partner because of her desire to acknowledge that bond and receive a reward. It's the kind of relationship we all admire and envy. And if we don't slip into replacing real training with forceful management and physical control of our dogs, we can have it.

According to Linda Eaton, assistance dog recipients come to the training center to learn about four key items:

1. How dogs learn: a general understanding of canine learning principles

2. Training techniques: how assistance dogs are trained at the center

3. Vocabulary: the verbal signals the dog has learned

4. Managing expectations: ensuring that the recipient maintains reasonable expectations about what the assistance dog can and can't do, and discussing the need for ongoing support of the dog's socialization and skills training to avoid a decline in skills

During the on-site training, the recipient is paired with a particular assistance dog. The handler and dog begin to work together as a unit. At the end of the training course, the handler and the dog have become a team and they graduate together. It's the start of a truly beautiful relationship!

"We want the dog to leave the center obedient, not just responsive to obedience commands," says Ann Hogg. What's the difference? The investment of the handler in the relationship with the dog and the dog's response to the depth of her handler's investment.

Elizabeth Broyles explains the importance of teaching recipients to keep their dog's socialization and behavior training keen. "Partners, especially those who don't get out of their homes much, should continue training and socializing their dogs or their dogs will lose the training eventually," she says. "Even our 'perfect' dogs require this support. Partners come back to the training center every two years for recertification training. We evaluate their dog's training history and answer their questions about handling their dogs. We encourage them to keep the dog's training sharp."

The companion dog owner can access this training information, too. A quick scan of the dog training books available from online booksellers or your local retailer will reveal a wealth of great books that explain, in detail, positive, reward-based dog training methods. These methods have replaced techniques designed to elicit canine obedience through harsh treatment and the threat of punishment. Contemporary dog training books provide step-by-step guides for teaching your dog basic, traditional behaviors such as "sit," "stay," "come," "down," and "heel." You can learn how to use a clicker, treats, toys, tricks, and games skillfully in your training activities.

You may opt to sign up for a basic obedience class for you and your dog. If you have implemented a solid socialization program with your dog, she will be ready and willing to enter a classroom with you. Not only will she be confident in this new environment, but she will have *learned how to learn* from her early socialization and training lessons. She will have learned that you have expectations about her behavior and will show her how to meet them.

Many undersocialized dogs entering dog obedience classes will be asked, for the first time, to transition from being physically managed and maneuvered by their owners to taking responsibility for their own actions. They will be required, for the first time, to learn self-discipline and to deliver requested new behaviors on their own. That's certainly a big leap for a beginner! The training that has been missing for these dogs is learning how to learn and take responsibility for their responses, which is different than merely learning to accept physical management from an owner. Many dogs never realize there's a specific behavior their owner is looking for when the owner gives them a particular signal. They haven't been trained to recognize signals or make sense of their meaning. Instead, they expect to be manipulated into whatever position or response their owner desires.

As a result of your work on your dog's socialization program, your dog has developed a mind-set that says, "I should pay attention to my owner for information about how I should act and what I should do. She will direct me and support me and reward me for doing the right thing. We will start out slowly and work up to challenges as I gain the necessary confidence and skills. She is my leader. I trust her judgment and know how to respond to her signals." Your socialized dog has established a mind-set that encourages and supports learning, giving you a head start in training for desired behaviors in an obedience class.

Assistance dog trainers use a unique set of canine behaviors and a corresponding vocabulary of signals not usually found in a basic dog training book. Some of these behaviors, like opening a drawer or picking up a dropped pen, may not be useful to a handler without a disability.

However, there is a treasure trove of behaviors and signals we can borrow from the assistance and therapy dog trainers, like "settle," "closer," "step," "visit," "up," careful," "look," and more, that offer the companion dog handler an enhanced degree of control and meaningful interaction with their dog. In addition, disabled handlers learn to use play, and especially the game of tug, in a way that many companion dog owners find helpful. We'll learn about these training "secrets" in this chapter.

PLAYING WITH TUG TOYS AS A TRAINING TOOL

Nancy Patriarco was visiting St. Francis, and I couldn't wait to watch her interact with the trainers, the puppy raisers, and their dogs. Nancy has worked her dogs in competitive obedience and herding for many years and is a highly respected trainer. Relaxed and soft-spoken, you get the impression that you are in the presence of a knowledgeable, kind, and caring training expert after just a few minutes in her company. Several assistance dog training centers have enlisted her aid to polish the behavior training skills of their training staff and puppy raisers.

On a beautiful sunlit afternoon, the St. Francis trainers and puppy raisers assembled in the center's outdoor training ring with Nancy to review the progress of their training and receive help with problem areas. After watching several of the puppy raisers work with their pups, Nancy talked about the usefulness of tug play in dog training.

From the sidelines, I asked Marilyn Wilson, who has instructed many group basic dog obedience classes, why dog owners are so reluctant to use toys as a training aid. On the first session of many of my own basic obedience classes, I have asked the owners to come to future classes with treats and a favorite toy to use as rewards for their dogs. The next week they dutifully arrive with a bag of yummy doggie treats, but almost always without a toy.

"Generally, people don't feel comfortable using the silly voices and behaviors that accompany play with their dogs in a group obedience class. [This comment immediately brought to mind a dog's natural desire to remain inconspicuous. People have it, too.] Also, owners haven't built the foundation for play as a reward for their dogs. They haven't taught the rules of play to their dogs before coming to class, so the play may get out of hand in a group setting. Most owners think they will be using treats and praise to teach behaviors to their dogs. Period. Play as a reward is outside the box and meets with some resistance. Using play as a reward is not within the expectations of handlers going to a beginner dog obedience class."

Marilyn continues, "Redirecting your dog's attention to you through play beats scolding to regain your dog's focus. Plus, tugging adds another potential reward to your training tool box, and it's a reward with lots of benefits. Dogs love a treat, but there is a letdown immediately after it's consumed. It's a short-lived reward. Petting and praise also function as rewards, but their effectiveness is very dependent on the individual dog. Some dogs hate being hugged or touched on the head. Others prefer gentle stroking to rough petting. You have to get it exactly right for your dog, or it can act against you. For some dogs, praise becomes a low-value reward after it is diluted by the owner when used improperly or too often. Play creates a bond between the dog and the owner and keeps the dog in an 'up' state even after the training activity is finished."

In my own experience, many handlers have told me they think tug play is too aggressive and encourages bad habits like keep-away, nipping, grabbing, and growling. Some believe it teaches the dog to apply her strength against her owner. They worry that playing tug might cause their dog to value winning over cooperation.

I listened to Nancy tell the puppy raisers why tug play training is so important for adult assistance dogs. "Tug, if trained and used properly, is a great reward and a ready tool to use when problems arise," she explained. "It helps your dog to avoid distractions and shows her that, regardless of the pressure or stress she may feel at the moment, she should stay closely connected with you."

Tug works especially well when there is not enough room to let a dog run off her pent-up energy or when the handler can't physically accompany the dog on a run to let off steam.

Partners usually carry a tug toy and use it to release tension in their dogs and redirect their attention to the partner. For instance, if a partner finds their dog's attention wandering while in the grocery store, they can stop and quickly play a bit of tug with the dog to refocus her on her handler. Then they can resume their shopping. If they notice the dog stiffen, clench her mouth shut, and drop her tail after the entire middle-school soccer team has hugged her and thumped on her at the park, they can release some of the dog's tension and refocus her by taking a moment to play tug.

Nancy (with the hat) and Marilyn watch a puppy
let off some steam by playing tug.

Nancy tells the puppy raisers how to teach the pups to play tug properly. First, show the dog the tug toy. If your dog shows no interest in it, play with it yourself. If she approaches you, gently push her away. "What you can't have, you want," Nancy explains.

When the dog shows interest in the tug toy, have her come in toward you to get the toy. Don't go toward your dog and push the toy at her. "That's teasing," says Nancy. "Your dog has to come to you to get the toy."

Start by telling your dog to "get it." Don't let your dog grab the toy and bring it to you. *You* start the game and allow her to have the toy on your signal by encouraging her to take it from your hand.

Have a super-tasty treat available. After a short game of tug, tell your dog to "give." Show your dog the treat. When she releases the tug toy, give her the treat, then *immediately give the tug toy back to her.* Play a few more rounds of tug in the same manner. Your dog will learn that giving you the tug toy when you ask for it will result in both a yummy treat *and* a continuation of the tug game. Stop the game after a few iterations of the training. End the game calmly and with lots of praise and treats. Put the tug toy away and keep it under your control. Use it as a special, high-value toy for tug games only.

If your dog decides not to give the tug toy to you when you ask for it, stop the game entirely, secure the toy calmly, quietly place the tug toy out of her reach, and walk away. No following the rules, no fun.

Nancy watches as a puppy learns to
calmly accept touches while playing tug.

Next, Nancy has the trainers touch the dog on her left and right sides while tugging. "This action pairs touch with tug and reinforces touch as a positive occurrence and even a reward for the dog," she says. "Assistance dogs will experience many touches in their careers, and they can't be insulted by them. They must learn to accept them." Later, Nancy shows the trainers how to thump the dog's side with their cupped hand while tugging. The dogs learn to gracefully accept a more assertive bump and remain upbeat and focused.

Pair tug with behavior training: tug and then practice "sit" for awhile; tug and practice "down"; tug and practice "back up." Tugging will help to keep your dog happy and upbeat throughout the training session.

In a progression similar to the steps I discussed in the socialization program outlined in chapter 7, Nancy advises the trainers to practice playing tug outside in "easy places" such as parking lots and parks. Next, practice tug at the *approaches* to "difficult places" (busy indoor locations), like on the steps leading into the public library or outside the automatic doors at the pharmacy. Finally, practice controlled tugging indoors in the supermarket or in the doctor's office. Each step requires the dog to interact and focus on the handler under more stressful and distracting conditions.

You will not have access to most indoor locations to work with your companion dog, but you can work in the homes of your friends and family. Arrive early for dog obedience class and practice tug inside the training center before class begins. "Now," says Nancy, "if something alarms your dog, you can always tug and redirect her attention to you."

I use tug all the time at agility trials. My two Border Terriers are highly reactive dogs, and they must queue up at the start line with a bunch of other eager, jazzed-up dogs. It's close quarters, especially in warm, sunny weather when the handlers are all trying to get their dogs under the shade tent near the start line and keep them cool before their run. In particular, Chase, who is reactive *and* protective of his personal space, must learn to accept milling dogs and handlers all around him while mentally getting ready to run the course. He gets bumped and jostled by other dogs, many of whom are equally worried about the conditions (especially the Shetland Sheepdogs, a herding breed who run in the same group as Chase, and who, it appears, are always thoroughly disgusted by this disorganized gaggle of dogs that is entirely out of their control!).

Treats and toys are not permitted within ten feet of the agility ring in almost all agility trials. When I release Chase from his kennel, I give him his tug toy. He knows he's about ready to have a run, so his pupils are the size of salad plates and he's already in high gear. I play with him in our set-up area for just a few seconds and then proceed to the ring. I can feel him direct his energy to the tugging. We walk to the ring still tugging mildly. If a wild-eyed dog who has just completed his run comes darting by us, I know Chase will stay on the tug toy and out of trouble. We get closer to the ring, and he stays latched on to the toy. Terriers often eviscerate their prey, so sometimes I let Chase take the tug toy (a braided flannel strip about eighteen inches long). He will hold it on the ground with his front paws and pull at it with his teeth.

I am careful to tug more enthusiastically in our set-up area and keep the game under tighter control closer to the start line so as not to overstimulate the other dogs. Chase remains almost oblivious to the crowded conditions and is releasing some pent-up stress. Many times Chase merely keeps his jaws clamped down on the toy without tugging at all, and watches the other dogs running in the ring (it looks like he's trying to get in his "zone"). I encourage him to do so, because he remains physically connected with me (I'm at the other end of the toy!) and I can feel so much of his mental state communicated from his mouth through the toy to me. Just before our turn arrives, I softly ask for the tug toy, give him a treat or a pet for releasing it, stash the tug toy away from the ring, and move to the start line, leaving the crowd behind.

Using a tug toy with Chase in this way keeps me connected with him without activating his opposition reflex. Most mammals tend to pull against pressure to move forward; they do not automatically surrender to it. That's why the harder you pull on your dog's leash, the more she resists. Remember those scenes in the old Western movies where the prospector is pushing his supply-laden donkey from the rear, only to have the animal lean far back and dig in hard to maintain his position? No one gets anywhere. Try it yourself. If someone approaches you, suddenly grabs your hand, and pulls you forward, will you follow instantly or hesitate and hold back? (I also know some people who have very well-developed *mental* oppositional reflexes!)

If I were using Chase's leash to physically maneuver him through the crowded ringside conditions, he would naturally tighten against the leash and we would find ourselves in an oppositional mode. Not a good state of mind with which to start an agility run. With his tug toy firmly in his mouth and his leash hanging loosely, he walks with me to the ring, prancing all the way. He's about to engage in his favorite activity, and he's pumped. I have control of his head (I have the other end of the tug toy in my hands), so I can read him and govern his movements with a light touch.

I have used subdued tugging in crowded veterinarians' waiting rooms and as a reward after a particularly tiring training session. Just be sure that you protect your dog from others nearby who might want to challenge him for his interesting tug-toy treasure.

"Tugging helps your dog to stay in the moment, even when it's hard," Nancy tells the puppy raisers. She adds, "Don't be too worried about what worries your dog. Cut yourself loose from his emotions and let him handle the situation using the tools you have given him. Be there to support him when necessary."

UM, SHOULD I TAKE THAT AS A YES OR A NO?

As with all endeavors devised by humans, we tend to take dog training, and its varied philosophies, to extremes. Decades ago, the world of dog training was filled with punishments like slapping, rubbing noses in excrement, yelling, leash jerking, and banishment from the family to the basement or the backyard (solitary confinement). The advent of positive training methods brought treats, praise, clickers, play, and lures onto center stage, and banished aversives from the scene. Many of today's dog trainers who use positive training methods *never* use aversive signals or negative reactions with their dogs. Their responses to their dogs' behaviors consist only of providing a reward for correct behavior and simply ignoring an unwanted behavior, which they expect will fade away if they don't reward it. The issue is controversial and complex.

"If you train totally without the use of aversives," says Nancy, "the dog does not learn how to handle them in real life." Again, with the goal of fully socializing assistance dogs, Nancy wants the dogs to maintain their composure even if someone gently corrects them (no harsh treatment should ever befall an assistance dog or any dog). "Also, some dogs need to know quickly whether they were right or wrong," she continues. "It builds confidence in the relationship with the handler when the dog does not have to wonder if her choices were correct or not. She knows her handler will advise her in a caring way." We can't assume that rewards, or lack of rewards, coming from us are the only source of conditioning for our dogs. Dogs can engage in inappropriate behaviors, like stealing food or chasing squirrels, that are self-rewarding and do not require any input from the owner to be gratifying to the dog. If you don't correct these behaviors, they will continue anyway based on their self-rewarding nature. These unwanted behaviors will not extinguish on their own, but will flourish because they are self-rewarding.

"The dogs deserve to know what their limitations are," says Kali Kosch. "We use verbal indicators like 'wrong' and 'no' that serve as corrections, but we concentrate on training alternative behaviors right away. We don't stop at telling the dog, 'you can't do that.' We always add, 'do this instead.'"

Indicators that the dog is right (rewards) or wrong (corrections) are called "markers." Rewards, or positive markers, include petting, praise, treats, play, and valued activities such as running free in the yard or woods. Corrections or negative markers include simply the lack of a reward ("'the lack of information' can be used as a negative marker," says Ann Hogg), or a verbal "wrong" (good try, but no cigar!) or "no" (reserved for behaviors that are *never* tolerated).

The trainers teach new behaviors using lots of positive markers and few negative markers. After the trainer sees that the dog knows the behavior but either refuses to perform it or performs it incorrectly, they may consider using a negative marker to indicate the need for the dog to improve her response.

I watched Marilyn Wilson work with the puppy raisers, who were teaching their charges to keep their heads up and not sniff the ground. Remember that assistance and therapy dogs can't spend their time in food stores, hospitals, and subway stations constantly snuffling the ground, even though these places offer a smorgasbord of interesting aromas. First, Marilyn instructed the puppy raisers to discourage the dog's sniffing behavior by moving along at a faster pace, which makes sniffing more difficult, and by talking to their dogs, which keeps the dogs' heads up. The trainer marks and rewards the dog when her head stays up. If the dog persists with sniffing, the trainer *gently* taps the pup under the chin with the toe of their shoe (negative marker). The dog picks her head up and immediately receives a reward (positive marker).

Later, the trainers may use a careful correction when an experienced dog knows a behavior (without doubt) and is comfortable in the environment, but refuses to deliver the behavior. For instance, if a dog refuses to pick up a dropped article at home, the trainer might mark the mistake with "wrong," and then proceed to work through the problem. If the dog has not learned the behavior yet, there's nothing to correct because the dog doesn't know what to do.

When I play tug with Dash and signal her to "give," I will say "wrong" in a firm but conversational tone of voice if she refuses to release the tug toy quickly (which, on the rare occasion, she does). She has chosen the game over my signal to release: a wrong choice. When she hears my "wrong," she always releases the toy immediately. I have reminded her that she has made the wrong decision, and it will result in the cessation of play if she doesn't correct it right away.

Essentially, a dog may not deliver a requested behavior because her handler has not trained the behavior thoroughly or because the dog has not been socialized well enough to be able to put her training to use in an uncomfortable environment due to distractions, fear, or the desire to remain inconspicuous.

Let's face it. You don't always feel like doing everything someone else tells you to do. Neither do dogs. And it's not always a matter of not understanding what the other person wants you to do. Sometimes it's a matter of fatigue, confusion, worry, lack of confidence, shyness, or even pain. Sometimes the dog just feels like doing something in a certain way on the spur of the moment. However, you are more inclined to do something for a dear friend or a favorite family member, even if you are not in the mood to do it. You are less likely to extend yourself at the request of a casual acquaintance or a coworker you're not fond of anyway. One of the benefits of undertaking the socialization and training program outlined by the trainers in this book is that it transforms you, the handler, into a beloved leader in your dog's eyes. And that status greatly increases the dog's willingness to respond to you reliably.

It's a delicate balance between supporting the dog as she learns and advising the dog about the status of her conscious decisions when they are incorrect.

Choose and apply negative training markers carefully so that they enhance your relationship with your dog by providing additional, useful information to her. Socialize your dog so that she will be confident enough to deliver requested behaviors in many different environments. Do not misinterpret inadequate socialization as your dog's stubborn refusal to acknowledge your signals. Inadequately socialized dogs do not possess the skills to perform requested behaviors reliably in public. Their lack of performance should not earn them a negative marker.

THE POSITIVE BASICS

Follow these basic steps when teaching your dog new behaviors.

1. Create the behavior (catch the dog in the act, lure the dog into performing the behavior, or gradually shape the behavior).

2. Name the cue for the behavior.

3. Mark the behavior (click or say "yes" or "that's it").

4. Reward the behavior.

5. Release the dog from the exercise (say "OK").

Let's say you want to teach your dog to sneeze on cue. Wait until your dog sneezes naturally (catch the dog in the act). Say "sneeze" (name the cue), click your clicker or say "yes" (mark the desired behavior), and reward the behavior (treat, praise, tug, or whatever is rewarding for your dog). Then tell your dog the short exercise is over by saying "OK" (release the dog).

Now teach a simple "sit." Face your standing dog with a treat in your hand. Move your hand up and over your dog's head until she can't see the treat and she naturally sits (in other words, lure her into a sitting position using the treat). Say "sit." Mark the sit with a clicker or "yes." Reward your dog, then release her with "OK."

Teach your dog to shake hands. When your dog lifts her paw just an inch off the ground, mark the behavior (the first step in getting to the final behavior). Reward, then release. Then up the ante: When your dog lifts her paw two inches higher off the ground, mark this progression to the ultimate desired behavior of raising her paw to shake. Reward. Release. Do the same for each step your dog takes that's closer to the ultimate desired behavior of raising her paw high enough to shake (shape each incremental step in the progression to the final behavior). Don't name the behavior until your dog has learned the final behavior.

Use a negative marker ("wrong") only when your dog knows the request-ed behavior completely, is in comfortable and familiar circumstances, and then gets it wrong. "Wrong" is not a punishment, it's helpful information about the choice your dog has just made.

If you think about it, dogs also provide us with negative markers. In agili-ty, I may choose a particular handling maneuver, like a rear cross, to get my dog through a difficult sequence of agility obstacles. When we run the sequence, I may find that the rear cross maneuver inadvertently sent my dog in the wrong direction, causing us to be disqualified. I didn't notice the potential "trap" in the sequence, and I provided a poorly chosen directional cue to my dog. Her reaction (responding to my cue, which put her off-course) provided me with a negative marker: I made the wrong handling choice that time. File it under "lesson learned."

BEYOND SIT AND STAY

Here is a collection of nifty behaviors and their corresponding signals that assis-tance and therapy dog trainers draw from to enhance communication with their dogs. These particular behaviors and signals are rarely taught in basic obedience classes or discussed in training books, but you can use the basic training meth-ods described in the previous section to train them. I have incorporated many of them into my training vocabulary, which has broadened the scope of com-munication between my dogs and me and connected us even more strongly.

Don't

This prevents the dog from doing something she is *considering*; it's not for something wrong she has already done (use "no" for that). You've got to watch your dog and be able to anticipate her behavior (a very good habit to practice!) to use "don't."

When I release my dogs into the front yard and I see Chase *about to* lift his leg on the gardenias, I say "don't" before he gets fully into position. He stops, looks at me abashedly, and trots over to the stand of oak trees in the far corner of the yard to relieve himself. If an assistance dog spots an enticing piece of candy in a child's hand and looks like she might investigate the opportunity for a taste more closely, the trainer says "don't" to halt the behavior progression.

An amazing change occurs in your relationship with your dog when she discovers that you have eyes in the back of your head and can anticipate her moves. It builds respect and the trust that you are fully aware of what's going on around you and her, and that you always include her actions in your decisions.

Settle

Lydia says this signal means "relax and quit messing around." I use it all the time with Dash. She is a very energetic, busy little terrier, which I much admire. However, sometimes she drives me to distraction or doesn't modulate her behavior to suit the circumstances. When I land in my reading chair at the end of a busy day and she grabs her ball and pesters me to play, I tell her "settle." To her it means "no matter how much you try, I'm not going to play, so you should just cool it for now." She drops her ball and finds a bone to chew, having learned that persistence will not change things. This resolution beats having her hound me for thirty minutes straight, hoping that I will cave in and play, which only results in exasperation for both of us.

On our way to the agility ring, Dash tugs enthusiastically. However, I don't want her to join the concentration of dogs and handlers waiting to run while she's tugging wildly. It will disrupt the entire group. I signal her to settle as we approach the group, and she immediately scales it down to a quiet, subtle tug.

If you signal "settle" and wait patiently and quietly until your dog has stepped down her level of activity before proceeding, and *never* give in by escalating the activity level again once you have said it, your dog will learn this skill quickly.

Better Hurry or Hurry Up

Trainers use this signal to tell the dog to empty her bladder and bowels now. They don't always have time to wander around waiting for a dog to investigate the countryside before eliminating.

As your dog naturally eliminates, say "hurry up," and give her a treat. Take her out when you know she really has to eliminate right away and say "hurry up" just before she complies. Reward her. Practice this lesson on leash, too. You don't want a dog who will not eliminate unless she gets to run loose for awhile. Signal your dog to "hurry up," reward her, and then take a short walk or a playful romp. Don't reverse the order and play first, or your dog will pair the signal "hurry up" with the end of a fun trip outside and not the beginning. That will only encourage her *not to* hurry up.

Dash is almost comical in the way she squats and pees immediately when I say "hurry up." She knows that nothing else will happen until she's empty and she wants to get on with whatever fun activity is coming next!

Careful or Easy

Lydia's definition is that this signal cautions the dog to prepare for a precarious situation. It tells your dog to pay close attention. Draw out the word into long syllables when you say it to communicate a cautionary message to your dog. Your tone of voice will indicate your intention to your dog when you first use this signal, and your dog will come to recognize the word itself later.

Assistance dog partners use it when a dog is about to step onto an escalator or board a plane. I use it when my dog is running agility and is about to race onto the narrow up ramp of the dog-walk obstacle with paws wet from morning dew.

Closer

This means "move closer to me." I much prefer this signal to forcibly pulling my dog toward me with the leash. Partners use it before passing through tight spaces or while standing in line with their assistance dog. I use it when I'm walking with Chase and he spies another dog ahead in our path. When I say "closer" to Chase, it tells him, "I see the situation and I'll handle it. I've got it under control so just stay with me and be calm." Or, when I'm sitting ringside with my dog and another handler wants to squeeze her chair into the small space next to mine, I can tell my dog to move closer to me to make room.

Back

It means "step backward." It's hard enough negotiating a wheelchair through the checkout line at the grocery store or down the aisle in a movie theater, never mind trying to do so with an assistance dog at your side. Sometimes the dog has to follow behind her partner when they find themselves in close quarters. The trainers teach the dogs to step back behind the partner when signaled, using "back."

I use it when my dogs know we're going out to play ball and they rush to the door ahead of me. I signal "back," and they must step back away from the door and behind me or I will not open it. Period. I don't want to deal with chaos and a mad rush at the door. I also use "back" when another dog approaches us aggressively. I put my dog behind me as a signal to my dog that I'll take care of the problem and to tell the other dog "you'll have to go through me first if you are looking for a fight."

Move or Move It

This means "get out of the way." I prefer it to nudging my dogs with my foot or bumping them on their flanks with my leg. It signals that there's no place I particularly want you to be right now, as long as it's not *there*.

Step

About a million students have told me that their big, exuberant dog has dragged someone down their front stairs and injured that person. Assistance dogs are big, too, and are capable of creating the same outcome. Assistance dog trainers teach the dogs the signal "step," which means "take one step at a time, and don't take the next one until I tell you."

Start at the top of a set of two or three stairs with your dog on a leash. Proceed slowly. Take one step down with your dog, say "step," stop, mark the behavior with a click or "yes," and reward it. Repeat until you reach the bottom of the stairs. Release your dog.

Marilyn teaches "step" while a puppy raiser watches.

Marilyn praises the dog for holding
her position.

A puppy raiser tries her hand at
teaching her dog "step."

Look

Assistance dog trainers mentally check in with their dogs all the time using eye contact. Comfortable eye contact with your dog creates an instant, deep connection. However, it's unnatural for canines to maintain eye contact with another animal unless they are asserting themselves, so making eye contact to check in with their handler is a skill that owners must teach to their dogs. Use

Marilyn tries to entice a pup's attention from her handler with
some yummy cheese, but the dog stays focused on her handler.
Good work!

"look" to get your dog's attention focused on you, but always be available when
you ask your dog to "look."

Sometimes Chase gets so fixated on watching the dogs ahead of us run the
agility course that he seems to forget about me standing next to him. Agility is
a team sport; we do it together. He can't just race out onto the course and take
any obstacles he likes, although sometimes he looks as if that's just what he's
going to do. I remind him to connect with me by signaling "look" just before
it's our turn to run.

That's It

"That's it" is my favorite signal that I have borrowed from Lydia. It speeds up
the process of shaping a desired behavior. When Lydia wants to train an assistance dog to turn on a light switch, she uses a switch mounted on a board. She
shapes the behavior by rewarding the dog's incremental attempts as she gets
closer and closer to the ultimate, desired behavior. For instance, when the dog
lifts her paw slightly, Lydia marks, rewards, and releases. When she lifts her paw
higher, she marks, rewards, and releases. Lydia works on every little step—pawing toward the board, touching the board, touching the switch, scratching at
the switch, moving the switch—until she has shaped the behavior of turning
on the light switch in one step.

This process takes time, and Lydia has accelerated it using "that's it." She says, "It's a message of encouragement that means the dog is on the right track." So instead of stopping to mark, reward, and release the dog at each and every small step in the progression to the ultimate behavior, she uses "that's it" to move her dog through several small steps and then stops to mark, reward, and release after the dog accomplishes larger increments in the progression.

She may say "that's it" as the dog lifts her paw higher and higher and then reward generously when the dog actually touches the board. Then she may say "that's it" as the dog touches and paws at the board and reward when the dog has touched the switch. "That's it" does not mark the end of the training activity the way a reward does. Dogs familiar with "that's it" know that they have only completed a step in the process and they should stay tuned for more training ahead.

I use "that's it" whenever I want to reassure my dogs that they're on the right track. When Dash approaches a friendly dog calmly and remembers her manners, I tell her "that's it" in an encouraging tone. She knows I monitor her to be sure she's not too hyperactive in the company of new dogs. "That's it" assures her that she is not doing anything that will cause me to remove her from the interaction.

Visit

If an assistance dog stays nicely by her partner's side when a visitor approaches, the partner may indicate to the dog that it's OK to relax and greet the visitor by using the signal "visit." Greeting means keeping all four paws on the ground but wiggling, wagging, and smiling at will. "Visit" also indicates that the excitement of interacting with the visitor is not a precursor to a play session, so when the dog hears "visit," she knows that she can relax and be friendly, but she cannot let her excitement get out of hand. She will soon be called back to her partner's side.

I only use "visit" to indicate that my dogs are free to greet humans—not other dogs. I don't use it for releasing them to greet other dogs because their physical displays naturally will be different with dogs than with people. I can't ask them not to raise their paws off the ground or spin around in the process of greeting another dog.

Paws Up

Therapy dog trainers use this signal to encourage a dog to put her front paws up on a surface or on a willing person. Many animal lovers confined to a bed or a wheelchair want the visiting dogs to get as close to them as possible. The dogs place their front paws gently on the edge of the bed or on the person's lap and enjoy extra pats.

I use "paws up" to make putting a walking harness on my dogs easier. Standing in front of my dog, I signal "paws up." The dog places her front paws on my thighs, and I clip on the harness and release the dog with an "OK."

Sniff

Sniffing is an important indulgence for dogs, but most handlers don't appreciate it when their dogs sniff all the time, even though it's the dog's natural inclination. It slows down the pace of a walk and distracts the dog during training sessions. Therefore, most dogs have to be trained that sniffing is prohibited without permission.

There are times when you will want to let your dog just be a dog. Perhaps, during a walk or on a break during a therapy visit or an obedience class, your dog may want to indulge in a doggie behavior such as sniffing. You can allow her to do so as a type of reward or a way to relax. When walking with your dog, signal "sniff" and just let your dog collect all the wonderful odors present in her environment for awhile. It won't take long for her to learn that "sniff" means she can indulge in this important behavior, and she will take advantage of any opportunities you offer to her. I often catch a look sent in my direction by my dogs that says, "Thanks! This activity is wonderful! But by the way, what's the matter with you? Don't you smell all of these great aromas? Isn't your nose working? How can you resist sniffing the ground yourself?" I can only chuckle at their puzzlement and allow them to enjoy this very doggie behavior on their own.

THERAPY DOG HANDLERS TEST THE WATERS (AND FIND THEMSELVES IN THE DEEP END OF THE POOL)

Developing this extended vocabulary to use with your dog, coupled with a history of black-belt socialization, will provide you with a mutual connection that surpasses the power of physical restraints such as tie-outs, barricades, and choke-chain collars. Leashes become backup safety devices and not the principal means of controlling your dog.

Want to test the strength of this invisible connection linking you and your dog? Want to test the effectiveness of the special signals that assistance and therapy dog trainers use in their training programs and that you have taught your dog? Let's join Jan Stice's therapy dog training class in progress and see how her handlers fare.

Tonight is one of the later sessions in the course, and the seven handlers and their dogs have practiced many aspects of therapy dog visits in an institutional setting. All the participants are gathered in the training room when Jan asks Jeanie to bring out the supplies for the next exercise from the storage room. Jeanie returns to the training area with seven pieces of black yarn, each about four or five feet long. Jeanie gives a length of yarn to each handler, and Jan instructs the handlers to remove the leashes from their dog's collars and replace them with a piece of yarn tied to the collar. Then, she announces, they will proceed with the rest of the exercises planned for the class.

For a moment, the group is stunned into complete silence (Jan is enjoying this reaction entirely too much!). When the handlers realize Jan is serious about her request, they comply.

Obviously, the yarn provides no physical control over the dogs at all. It acts solely as a fragile line of connection and a way for the handlers to keep their hands occupied and off their dogs. Jan doesn't want the handlers hovering over the dogs and grabbing at the dogs' collars at every step to gain control now that their leashes are gone.

As soon as the leashes hit the floor, the chatter in the room explodes. Each handler now may rely only on gestures and verbal signals to manage their dog. Handlers who had spoken to their dogs only occasionally during the beginning of the class now direct a veritable monologue at their dogs, complete with requests for regular eye contact and the generous dispensing of treats to retain their dog's focus. The dogs, sensing that their restraints have been lightened and their handlers have somehow instantly been transformed into animated chatterboxes, are on high alert. Seeing this change in their dogs' demeanor, of course, increases the anxiety level of the handlers, who up the noise level in the room even more. Jan is still having much too good a time observing this metamorphosis!

Jan asks the handlers to run their dogs through a few simple obedience commands. They practice "sit" and "down" and "stay" while standing in place. Jan watches as handlers automatically start to work the yarn "leash" to bring their dogs under control, then remember its flimsy nature and quickly switch to verbal signals and gestures. Soon the dogs settle down and the handlers generally receive the responses they want from the dogs.

Jeanie circles around the group, walking behind the teams while holding a ball in her hands to test each handler's ability to keep their dog in place without physically restraining the dog. Then she walks beside each dog and gently bumps the dog on the flank as she passes. Will the dog spin around and startle at the touch or can the handler keep the dog focused using tools other than a leash? The handlers work to keep their dogs' attention, and the dogs receive rich rewards for their good behavior.

Now Jan announces that the dogs and handlers will start moving. The teams form a circle in the training area, with each dog sitting next to her handler. At a brisk pace, one team at a time weaves through the waiting teams, around the circle, and returns to their original place. As soon as a team goes into motion the decibel level of the voices in the room ratchets up another few notches. Waiting handlers speak to their dogs to keep their attention while the walking dog passes by. The walking handler gushes a stream of verbal signals. At the conclusion of the exercise, the handlers are exhausted and the dogs are a bit wild-eyed.

One dog becomes overly excited and the handler cannot keep her under control using the yarn leash. Jan motions the dog and handler away from the training area to a quieter corner. She instructs them to relax for a few minutes, then they can rejoin the class with a regular leash on the dog. The handler will practice this training at home, and the team will try the exercise again with the yarn leash at the next class.

After all the handlers have leashed up their dogs once again, they share a hearty laugh and shake their heads as they discuss the exercise. Many of them hug their dogs or reward them with a good game of tug or several high-value treats, as up-beat now as they were surprised earlier. They sense how connected they have become as a team and how far they have yet to go to replace physical control with training.

Could you walk your dog on a yarn leash successfully?

It's really difficult to forsake the traditional leash for the invisible bond composed of verbal communications, body language, and reward-based training. It's tough to replace the effectiveness of hands-on physical management of a dog with the tenuous connection of a relationship. It's hard work to create a strong mental union with a dog when a simple leather strap is readily available.

"Avoidance and undemanding measures do not make good therapy dog training techniques," Jan remarks to me with a smile. Indeed.

TRAINING TIPS FROM THE PROS

Assistance and therapy dog trainers throw pearls of wisdom around like rice at a wedding. Here's a handful. Catch a few that can help you deepen the training relationship with your dog.

Give your dog a moment to think.

So many trainers expect instant compliance. They move much too quickly when teaching their dog a new behavior. Marilyn Wilson reminds the puppy raisers not to repeat signals when the dog does not respond immediately, especially during the initial training of a behavior. "Just wait a few seconds while the dog thinks about it," she says. "Then reward them when they do it. Later, you can work toward immediacy and speed."

Elizabeth Broyles told me about an assistance dog partner attending a recertification class. The partner complained that her assistance dog refused to step onto an escalator. Elizabeth and the team visited a shopping mall to practice the behavior. The dog had not experienced an escalator in quite a long time and the noise frightened her, but the partner became frustrated and pressured the dog hard to step onto the moving steps. Elizabeth reminded the partner to give the dog time to consider the challenge and become comfortable with it. After a few short lessons taken at the dog's natural pace, the dog willingly rode the escalator with her partner.

Use trick training to practice your timing skills.

Timing is important in dog training. Rewarding your dog in a way that truly identifies the behavior you desire takes practice. For instance, if you are teaching your dog "look" and she turns, makes eye contact, and then jumps on you for a treat, you may actually train her to jump up on you unless you mark and treat the "look" on time. Your dog pairs the reward with the behavior that most recently preceded it. You have to be quick to catch and mark the "look."

Work on fun tricks like "roll over," "play dead," "spin," or "speak" to practice your timing and get a feel for your dog's reaction time in the training environment. Then apply your knowledge to training more complex signals.

Involve the whole family to maintain consistency in the training.

Ann Hogg asks the puppy raisers to post a list of training signals and their meanings on the refrigerator at home. All family members use this vocabulary when interacting with the pup. The puppy raisers review the signals with their family members to be sure everyone supports, rather than contradicts, the training program.

Don't avoid weak points or problem areas.

I have to discipline myself all the time to practice the agility skills my dogs and I don't perform well. It's uplifting to go out and work with my dogs on skills at which we excel. The training session is thoroughly enjoyable, but it doesn't get us closer to qualifying the next time we run.

Some assistance dog partners place a strap on refrigerator and cabinet doors so that their dog can pull them open on their signal. However, one pup-in-training tugged on the strap whenever she saw it, trying to instigate a game of tug with the refrigerator. The puppy raiser cannot delay training the pup to tug only when signaled to do so. She must resolve the issue before the pup can progress in her training.

Avoid drills and patterns.

Mix it up to keep you and your dog fresh and engaged during each session.

Concentrate on teaching what to do, rather than on marking what not to do.

Because otherwise, no one is having any fun.

Add distractions after your dog has learned a behavior.

What is a distraction? "Anything that changes the picture," explains Nancy Patriarco. "It's amazing how little it takes." After a pup has learned "come" from about twelve feet away, the puppy raiser places a single toy in the dog's path and repeats the command. Soon, the pup is trotting through a pile of toys or weaving through a group of people to get to her handler.

Think of the training environment and its distractions in 360 degrees. Distractions don't always have to be something in the direct path of your dog. Dogs playing together in the distance may provide an unavoidable temptation for your dog, even when her direct path to you is completely empty of distractions.

Keep your training criteria stringent at first; loosen up later.

Many partners will not demand the level of performance from their dogs that the trainers require. The trainers expect that the dog's skills will become less precise as they continue their careers with their partners. If the trainers accepted approximate interpretations of their signals from the dogs at the training center, the dogs' lack of precision would become even greater later. Begin the training using precise criteria; give your dog a clear picture of exactly what you want her to do.

Preserve the value of the rewards.

Nancy says save high-value rewards (a special toy or treat) for training new behaviors, not for rewarding already known behaviors. Otherwise, the reward doesn't continue to have high value for the dog.

When planning to train a new behavior, start the session by reviewing behaviors the dog knows. Build on the success of her responses and her cooperative frame of mind to start training the new behavior. Bring out the high-value reward during this part of the training. "Don't pass out an array of treats, brought directly to your waiting dog, throughout the session. You're not the pizza delivery guy," quips Nancy. "Have your dog come to you to receive her occasional high-value reward."

Keep it quiet.

Nancy cautions the trainers not to overstimulate their dogs during training. "Dogs, like people, don't learn well when they are overly excited."

Know how to go backward as well as forward to find solutions.

When a training session is not progressing well, or a new technique does not provide the response you are looking for from your dog, go back to what works and to where your dog is comfortable. Approach the training from a different direction. Break the training steps down into smaller segments to make conquering each one easier for your dog. Find a new path to success.

Don't be afraid of making a mistake.

Failing to socialize and train your dog at all is a far more serious error than bungling a training session or a socialization outing.

Establish training goals.

Unlike the assistance dog trainers, you have all the time in the world to work your training program. But you will need more than time to accomplish your training goals. A training program requires time *and* planning. The assistance dog trainers achieve an amazing amount of training in ten to thirty minutes of training a day, conducted four to six days a week. They plan their sessions and establish specific goals, which keeps them focused.

Create a scenario in which all good things in your dog's world come from you.

Play, treats, walks, social events, swims, interactions with other dogs, reward-based training, canine sports, pets, praise, privileges, dinner—all the good things in your dog's life should originate from you. You become the person to please in order to get access to goodies.

If your dog establishes her own access to enjoyable things, your position is reduced to a mere co-inhabitant of the house or even to a competitor. If your dog spends hours in the yard amusing herself by digging and barking at passers-by, if she runs loose and happily meets up with stray dogs or jumps in the creek for a swim at will, if she gets to sleep on the bed even if she snaps at a family member, then you have lost your ace card: you're no longer the one to please and the source of all things good. But play your hand right and you will create a companion dog who will give to you joyfully at least as good as she will get in return. It's a great deal, but you *both* have to learn to play your cards smart.

Chapter 9

Evaluating Socialization
Opportunities

My friend and fellow dog club member recently acquired a male terrier puppy. She and I both own adult terriers who have not been socialized in the manner described in this book and whom we must manage carefully when they are in contact with other dogs and in challenging environments. Both of our adult dogs protect their personal space and are not skilled in interpreting or communicating with other dogs during close encounters. They don't read the intentions of other dogs clearly and they escalate their own reactions to other dogs too quickly. They both assume the worst and act accordingly.

My friend decided that her new puppy would receive the early socialization necessary to produce a well-balanced adult dog with the ability to interact skillfully with other dogs and people. We both travel with our dogs, for pleasure and to participate in dog sports, so her puppy needs to be exposed to lots of different environments where she can teach him about handling himself with decorum.

My friend works in a demanding full-time job, but decided that early socialization was a critical factor in preparing her new puppy for his next ten to fifteen years as a member of her family. She put a temporary hold on some of the other requirements on her schedule and selected several socialization activities. She enrolled her pup in three weekly puppy kindergarten classes. One of the classes met at our club's training facility, and she registered her pup in two additional group classes taught by local private instructors. Also, she arranged to visit privately with club members who have nicely socialized and skilled dogs in their homes. She and the owners allowed the dogs to interact under their close supervision. She also made it a habit to take her new puppy out with her whenever it was safe and practical to do so. Now *that's* black-belt puppy socialization!

The result? A young dog with the social skills few adult dogs ever master. After three months of dedication to the task, my friend resumed her normal dog training schedule with the pup: one class a week, occasional play visits with friends, and trips outside the home and to events whenever possible. This week, the family headed out for their annual fall beach weekend, the puppy included.

My friend has laid a solid foundation for a take-anywhere companion dog. She can build lots of things on this foundation, such as an agility competitor, a therapy dog, an obedience competitor, a tracking dog, or simply a well-rounded member of her family. And the socialization that is the dog's foundation will strongly support it all.

Family dog training has blossomed into an array of businesses that offer everything from puppy kindergarten classes to doggie daycare to off-leash dog play centers to private obedience training and instruction. But as the assistance and therapy dog trainers have taught us, socializing and training your dog properly is important, and using inappropriate methods can backfire and work against your dog's progress.

Let's look at how to evaluate puppy and adult dog socialization and training opportunities to be certain they provide the high-quality learning experiences you desire for you and your dog.

PUPPY KINDERGARTEN GROUP CLASSES

Many owners think of puppy kindergarten classes as beginner obedience classes for very young dogs. But that's not the case. Puppy kindergarten classes and dog obedience classes should have very different objectives.

In puppy kindergarten classes, the focus of the training is *outward*, in an attempt to socialize the pup to many SOAPs. The class provides you with the opportunity to teach your puppy how to handle himself in new and challenging environments. Class meets in a room or an outdoor location full of new smells and objects. The instructor may use props that you might find in a child's play yard, like a plastic slide, a fabric tunnel, or large building blocks. Children's toys that make noise (like the timeless lawn-mower-style push toy filled with clanking objects) or pop up (like a jack-in-the-box) add challenges. Many instructors bring refrigerator-size cardboard boxes, lawn chairs, floor mats with varied surfaces, and other training tools to class. People and dogs who are strangers to your pup fill the sessions and will interact with your dog closely. All of the SOAPs come together in this learning event.

You will learn to support your pup as he negotiates environmental challenges and interacts with people and dogs. The instruction focuses on the dog's ability to maintain his confidence, build his social skills, and recover his sense of decorum quickly in this world full of surprises—all with your support.

The instructor may include some simple obedience exercises in the curriculum, like "sit" or "down." They also will discuss how to handle unwanted behaviors before they become habits. But the main event remains socialization.

Basic or beginner dog obedience classes focus *inward* on the dog-owner relationship. In obedience class, your dog will learn to perform requested behaviors *despite* distractions from the environment, which he will learn to ignore. Once your dog has learned to handle challenges from the environment and recover quickly from particularly stimulating ones, he will learn to stay closely connected with you and offer behaviors confidently in the face of these challenges. So in obedience classes, instructors will provide environmental distractions for your dog while you maintain his focus on you and on the task at hand.

The approaches are polar opposites but are sometimes confused with one another.

When I teach a beginner obedience class for my dog club, I can spot in no time the dogs who have graduated from a puppy socialization class or who have been well socialized by their owners. Inadequately socialized dogs are so excited by the classroom environment that it's all their owners can do to physically restrain them from leaping around the room. The dogs barely give their owners a glance during the entire hour. They have not learned to rely on their owners for support and direction. The distractions mentally overwhelm the dogs and subvert their ability to learn and deliver new behaviors.

The socialized dogs are interested and attentive, but also responsive to their owners, and they look before they leap. They have learned to pause and take a tiny slice of time to evaluate a situation and compose themselves before taking action. They have learned to keep the communication channel open with their owners, even in this distracting setting.

Talk to the instructor of a puppy socialization class you are considering attending. Observe classes already in session, if possible. Keep the following criteria in mind when you select a puppy socialization class for you and your dog.

- Be sure the instructor organizes the puppy classes around the goal of socialization and not around beginner obedience training.
- Be sure the instructor monitors on-leash and off-leash interactions between puppies in the class carefully, whether two dogs or ten dogs are

playing together. Do they watch for bullying, cringing, aggressiveness, nipping and biting, chasing, hiding, crying and yelping, and do they take action to control these unproductive interactions?

- Be sure the instructor provides lots of time-outs for the puppies. After about five minutes of hard playing, puppies start to get tired and grumpy. Suddenly, the pups begin to nip harder, box with each other, run each other down, and pile on to the "softest" member of the group. That's not productive activity. Look for a class where play interactions are arranged in small increments with a chance to rest and recover in between. A class where puppies engage in unstructured play in a large group for twenty or thirty minutes at a time may encourage aggression rather than self-discipline. Never hesitate to remove your dog from a playgroup if the situation becomes too intense, and allow him to collect himself before he returns.

- Be sure your puppy will have the opportunity to interact with dogs of all sizes and breeds.

- Be sure the instructor teaches the owners how to read and interpret canine body language in their own dogs and in others. Be sure they advise their students how to communicate with their dogs, and with other dogs, using these same signals.

- Be wary of instructors who declare, "This is the way to do it, no matter how your pup reacts."

- Be sure the instructor provides direction about how to continue with socialization activities on your own between class sessions.

- Be sure the instructor teaches the students to use rewards and good handling practices to manage their puppies, as opposed to maneuvering the puppies around by dragging them on a leash. For instance, if your puppy is playing with several other puppies and you want to call him out of the group, you can move in, snap on his leash, and physically drag him away with you. Or you can have a high-value treat or toy available, call him name, lure him out of the play group, and reward him generously. Then, *immediately allow him to return to the play group*, so he will learn that coming to you does not mean the fun ceases. He will voluntarily come to you in the future.

- Be sure the instructor arranges for well-socialized adult dogs to visit the class and interact with each puppy. Members of my dog club often bring their well-behaved and especially puppy-tolerant dogs to one or two puppy classes in each session. Skilled adult dogs can teach the puppies about canine-to-canine interactions better than owners, instructors, and other puppies combined.

- If you can find a puppy socialization class for the public taught by an assistance or therapy dog trainer, enroll in it! You have found a Jedi Master of puppy socialization.

I spoke to one adult dog socialization class instructor who told me about homework she gives to her students. She teaches them how to take their dogs out and about on socialization trips and then asks the owners to take pictures of their dogs while in new settings, meeting new animals and people, and investigating unfamiliar objects, and then bring the photos to the next class. The students pass the pictures around and the owner describes the socialization experience. Other students comment on things like, "Your dog's ears are way back on his head and his posture is pushed backwards. He looks very concerned about being at the ball game," or "Look how nicely your dog is playing with that smaller dog." In this way, everyone benefits from these exchanges, even though they can't be together as a group when the training occurs.

OBEDIENCE TRAINING GROUP CLASSES

Socialization is not finished after puppy kindergarten ends (but you already knew that!). It's a lifelong undertaking that requires regular polishing to keep it bright.

Socialization becomes the foundation on which behavior training is built in obedience classes. Unfortunately, many owners expect their dog will acquire socialization through osmosis when they take him to an obedience class. Later, they find that the class does not focus on social skills, but on teaching and signaling behaviors, and their dog's lack of social skills diminishes the effectiveness of the obedience training.

Talk to the instructor of an obedience class you are considering attending. Observe classes already in session, if possible. Keep the following criteria in mind when you select an obedience class for you and your dog.

- Look for an instructor who helps their students extract the most benefit from classes by addressing socialization issues as well as teaching obedience methods.
- Look for an obedience instructor who encourages continued adult dog socialization outside the obedience classroom.
- Look for an obedience instructor who uses positive, reward-based training methods that are designed to build a strong human-canine relationship.

- Look for an obedience instructor who teaches that control of your dog originates from the strength of your relationship, not from your ability to physically manage your dog. Select an instructor who places leashes, collars, and harnesses in the category of "safety devices" and not in the category of "steering devices."

- Look for an instructor who encourages each owner to observe and know their own dog as an individual. Be wary of instructors who supply regimented lists of training exercises without an explanation of how they apply to your specific dog.

- Look for an instructor who is less interested in what all the dogs can learn to do and more interested in how each dog and owner can improve as a team.

OFF-LEASH DOG PARKS AND PLAY CENTERS

Many communities offer fenced areas in their parks where dogs may freely exercise and interact off-leash. A training center in my area has opened a members-only, off-leash, outdoor play center on their property. Owners pay an annual fee and the training center evaluates each dog for general fitness to join a play group. Upon approval, the dog may participate in the small dog play group or the large dog play group.

By providing off-leash play opportunities, owners anticipate that the dogs, unencumbered by leashes, will experience the joy of playing with other members of their own species and will be able to exercise vigorously. Some owners also use these sessions as socialization opportunities. But beware. Like any tool, owners should use these parks and play centers with caution.

Kali Kosch told me she brought one of her dogs to an off-leash dog park and left the site in less than five minutes. "They can be problematic," she said.

In a seminar about reading canine body language, I watched a video of a group of about eight dogs playing together, off-leash, in a large field. All the owners were present. The dogs were running around and chasing each other, and the owners were chatting and walking along with the dogs. The dog interactions were happening quickly and, before you could blink, one dog annoyed another dog one time too many and a serious fight erupted. Teeth flashed and one dog grabbed another hard. The owners panicked, dancing around the foray, all trying not to get bitten but eager to separate the dogs. After a few seconds of pandemonium, thankfully, the dogs parted and incurred only very slight injuries. The owners leashed the dogs and left the field shaken. The large size of the field, which gave the dogs the feeling that they had plenty of space in which to retreat, contributed to the fact that the incident did not engulf the entire canine group and to the relatively benign conclusion to this scary event.

The seminar instructor explained that, if you watch the video closely, the dogs had displayed body language signals that the play was becoming intense and that one particular dog was repeatedly annoying another dog. The annoyed dog had clearly escalated his warnings about his feelings before he resorted to a physical attack to stop the other dog's persistent behavior. However, no handlers were watching the dogs as the scene unfolded.

Personally, I don't find dog parks beneficial, but I hear many comments from people who claim their dogs love the off-leash park. If you and your dog plan to participate in off-leash, dog-park play sessions, be sure the facility carefully follows some important guidelines.

- Provide plenty of room in the play area. Adjust the number of participants to the amount of space available. Don't create an environment where your dog feels he cannot escape an unwanted advance from another dog, but must stand his ground and defend his personal space.

- Safety first. Fences are a must, preferably with an airlock design, which is a double gate enclosure where an incoming dog enters through the first gate, which closes behind him, and then passes through the next gate into the play area. Supplies for owners to clean up after their dogs should be at hand. All owners should keep a leash on their person at all times. Fresh water and shade should always be available for the dogs.

- Appoint a skilled moderator who can read canine body language, preferably someone without a dog in the mix. The moderator can step in and referee the group before tensions flare up. Private off-leash play centers often schedule groups of dogs who know each other to play at specific times, and a trainer from their facility moderates the group.

- Don't spend your time interacting with the other owners. Watch your dog continuously and carefully, and be ready to step in immediately to diffuse trouble. Socialize with the other owners after the play session has ended and the dogs are tired and back on leash.

- Match your dog to an appropriate group. Evaluate the size, age, temperament, social-skill level, energy level, and training history of the other dogs and be sure your dog fits in. Evaluate the skill levels of the other owners and the amount of supervision they provide for their dogs. Select a group in which the behavior of both the dogs and the owners complements your training philosophy.

- Time the sessions to conclude well before the dogs become overtired, hot, and cranky.

- Without your dog, visit the off-leash group you are planning to join and observe the dynamics during a few sessions. Listen to your gut feeling about how your dog will experience the activity.

- Not all dogs enjoy off-leash play with dogs outside of their "pack." Read your dog's body language and don't force him to engage in dog park activity if he's at all reluctant to do so. My mother was certain that I would love to learn to play a musical instrument. She bought me a piano and encouraged me to take lessons. Let's just say that I was less than enthusiastic (apologies to musicians everywhere!). Finally, she relented, halted the lessons, and bought me the dog I always wanted. I was never happier. I bet something similar has happened to you, so you know how it feels when someone urges you to participate in a "fun" activity that's not appealing to you.

- Never bring a young puppy to the dog park. Aside from the threat of health hazards to your pup, whose immune system has not fully developed, the presence of groups of adult dogs, some large, some with questionable social skills, and some with little or no experience interacting with puppies, presents challenges much too sophisticated for a young puppy to handle. Socialize your young pup in small groups of dogs with whom you are well-acquainted.

DOGGIE DAYCARE

Today, owners who work away from home but want to enjoy the companionship of a dog have options other than leaving their dogs home alone all day. Doggie daycare centers are sprouting up everywhere and offer a stimulating environment for dogs to enjoy while their owners are away from home. But, as we know, dogs require more than basic maintenance to develop into fine companions. You don't want a doggie daycare center to undo all the hard work you have invested in socializing your dog.

Make sure the daycare center follows training and management practices that complement your own training philosophy. Use the criteria discussed earlier for off-leash play centers and classes to evaluate doggie daycare centers. You will not be attending your dog's socialization and training sessions to monitor the appropriateness of the interactions, so you must be extremely cautious about handing over your precious puppy to their care.

When I worked in a corporate office, I hired a canine caretaker to visit my home once or twice during the day to let my dogs out in the yard and exercise them for a few minutes.

THERAPY DOG TRAINING CLASSES

Even if you have absolutely no plans to do therapy work with your dog, consider joining a therapy dog training class in your area. The trainers have an incredible amount of experience in evaluating the individual characteristics of dogs and handlers, and shaping socialization events and training exercises to their specific needs. They can tune up your ability to read canine body language and teach you how to engage those eyes in the back of your head.

They reign as the professors of positive training methods, and their classes qualify as university-level courses in relationship-based canine training. These trainers can provide you and your dog with the canine equivalent of a higher education.

AMERICAN KENNEL CLUB CANINE GOOD CITIZEN PROGRAM

In 1989, the American Kennel Club (AKC) initiated the Canine Good Citizen (CGC) program to recognize purebred and mixed breed dogs who demonstrate proper companion-dog behavior in the community, thereby serving as role models for others. Puppies can participate in the training and certification tests after they have received their immunizations. The AKC suggests that dogs who certify as puppies be retested when they reach adulthood, because canine behavior changes over time.

The AKC's web site has materials designed to assist dog owners with training to prepare their dog for CGC certification, but most obedience training centers and private instructors offer CGC preparation classes.

The CGC program is a two-step process. First, the owner signs the *Responsible Dog Owner's Pledge,* which says the owner provides for the health, safety, and quality-of-life needs of their dog while displaying responsible dog ownership in public.

The second part of the CGC program consists of a ten-part test performed under the direction of a certified CGC instructor.

1. Accept a friendly stranger.

2. Sit politely for petting.

3. Appearance and grooming.

4. Out for a walk on a loose lead.

5. Walk through a crowd.

6. Sit and lie down on command; stay in place.

7. Come when called.

8. Reaction to another dog.

9. Reaction to distraction.

10. Supervised separation (your dog must be left with the friendly tester for three minutes while you are out of sight, without continually barking, whining, pacing, or attempting to flee).

The owner may not physically force their dog into position, such as pushing them down on the floor after signaling "down." Neither may the owner constantly restrain the dog with a tight leash. Dogs must greet other dogs politely (testers use experienced, well-socialized, and trained dogs in the tests) and not panic in the face of distractions or when the owner leaves him for a short time.

Sound familiar? If you have followed the program shared with us by the assistance and therapy dog trainers, the test should be a no-brainer for you and your dog.

Even if you are not interested in collecting titles or certificates for your dog, classes that prepare participants for the AKC CGC test offer an opportunity for young and adult dogs to practice social skills and behaviors. They are worth your time for this benefit alone.

EVERYDAY LIFE IN SMALL DOSES

All these socialization and training opportunities are designed to put your dog under controlled pressure. The pressure may originate from the presence of other dogs or unfamiliar people, unique settings, scary objects, variable weather conditions, invasions of personal space, the need to perform reliably in the face of distractions, travel, loss of contact with the owner, noises, and more. In other words, they administer controlled dosages of everyday life in portions that result in improved performance, but not in portions that result in degraded performance arising from fear or excessive stress.

Your dog relies on you, his partner, to orchestrate these experiences in a way that supports his education.

Soon, your dog will become an old hand at managing his own behavior in these different circumstances and will recover quickly from newly stressful ones. You will have dispensed the most potent inoculation you can provide for your dog: emotional stamina. It's his most valuable life skill.

As you read this book, you may wonder why assistance dog trainers devote so much attention to supporting the dogs throughout their training when the whole point of having assistance dogs in the first place is for the dogs *to support people*. Sometimes when I listened to the trainers talk to their puppy raiser classes about supporting the dogs during the various training exercises, I felt like I was in an upside-down world because I had expected to hear a lot of talk about how the dogs will support their human partners.

But I had placed the chicken before the egg. Only dogs who have attained confidence, and what I think of as "social sophistication," can carry out their duties as partners to disabled persons. And these skills are developed only with the support of thoughtful and caring training.

The same is true for family dogs. Dogs who have achieved the level of sophistication that results from serious socialization and relationship-based training are positioned to take on life with their family in all its many facets.

Chapter 10

Developing the Deep Relationship

Jan Stice and her students have worked hard to prepare to take the Delta Society Pet Partners Skills Test and the Pet Partners Aptitude Test. Upon the successful completion of these tests, the teams will have Delta Society certification to participate in animal-assisted activities and therapy. Tonight, Jan has set up a simulated portion of a test in class so the teams can practice demonstrating the required skills.

Jan's husband and training assistant is seated in a wheelchair in the middle of the training room, positioned at a small table. A dessert plate and fork rest on the table. A large piece of cake sits on the plate, with a couple of pieces of cake scattered across the tabletop and several more tidbits of cake dropped on the floor around the wheelchair. Jan has placed items on the floor around the perimeter of the room, including towels soaked with iodine and alcohol, cotton balls sprayed with urine, and a few sugar pills laid in a pile.

On any pet therapy visit to a nursing home, a team might encounter any or all of these elements. A room may contain towels, bedding, articles of clothing, bandages, or other items that have a strong odor. Some items may have a particularly intense smell. The dogs, with their keen sense of smell, must be able to work in this environment without becoming distracted by or attracted to these odors. Remember that dogs use urine marking to communicate with other members of their species, so they don't find the smell of urine as obnoxious as humans do. Rather, they find it interesting. The dogs may try to investigate the smell more closely, which is not permitted in a therapy visit.

191

When the team visits residents in a common-room setting, they may encounter people eating a meal or snacking. There may be crumbs on a person's lap or hands or the floor. A resident or staff member may have dropped a pill or capsule on the floor. For the purposes of the training, Jan uses harmless sugar pills. However, during a real therapy visit, dangerous prescription drugs might accidentally end up under a bed or chair or in a corner. The dogs will be required to remain focused in the presence of these odors, foods, and medicines.

I watched as several handlers walked their dogs around the room, one at a time. Jan's husband called to each dog and asked, "Do you want a piece of cake?" The handlers told their dogs "don't" if they seemed about to take advantage of this offer, although the handlers continued to smile pleasantly. As the dogs passed by the items with the strong odors, the handlers watched their dogs, cautioned them when necessary, and rewarded them when they simply noted the item and moved on without incident. Jan observed each team carefully.

One handler and dog team entered the training area and Jan's husband immediately cooed, "What a cute dog! May I pet him? Would you like a piece of cake, doggie?" The handler smiled warmly and turned to talk to the man. She answered, "My dog can't eat cake but he would enjoy meeting you. How are you today? What's your name? Are you eating cake for a special occasion? Is it your birthday?" While the handler kept up this friendly dialogue with Jan's husband, her dog walked to the end of his leash, sniffed the nearby pile of pills, licked several up into his mouth, and swallowed them. When the handler felt her dog pull at his leash to snatch up a few more pills, she whirled around and, realizing what had occurred, exclaimed, "Oh no!"

I turned to Jan and said, "Obviously that constitutes a failure of the test."

"Yes, it does," Jan answered.

"Too bad; the dog was doing so well," I added.

"No, you've got it wrong," Jan said. "This instance was not a failure of the dog. It was a failure of the *handler*. The dogs are not required to enter this type of environment and do things like disregard pills on the floor entirely on their own. They're required to disregard pills on the floor *when told to do so*. It's the handler's responsibility to perform the therapy visit and be available to support and guide their dogs every second of the time. You cannot place pleasing the residents before the safety of your dog, although it's easy to lose focus when everyone wants your attention and clamors to spend time with your dog. You feel that the point of your visit is to cheer these people up, so you focus on that work. But you can't let your attention slide away from your dog in this potentially harmful surrounding. This test is more a test of handlers watching out for their dogs in the therapy environment than it is of dogs knowing what to do on their own."

I was reminded again of the nature of the deep relationship that assistance and therapy dog trainers and partners aspire to develop with their dogs—an invisible but strong connection that binds the dogs and trainers together, each constantly in mental touch with their partner despite distractions.

I received another reminder when I turned on the *Today* show one morning a few weeks ago. Meredith Vieira was interviewing a lovely and articulate young lady named Shea Megale about her new book titled *Marvelous Mercer*. Twelve-year-old Shea, confined to a wheelchair, suffers from spinal muscular atrophy. Her assistance dog, a black Labrador Retriever named Mercer, and her mother, accompanied her to the interview. Shea dreamed each night about adventures that Mercer had but that she could not participate in because of her disability, and kept a journal filled with stories of Mercer's imagined escapades. Her mother had discovered the journal and encouraged her daughter to publish it.

During the interview, Vieira asked Shea what things Mercer did to help her. Shea began to list items like "pick up what I drop" and "pull open doors for me." Suddenly she stopped, looked at Vieira, and said that, in truth, she had an entire family to do those things for her. What Mercer did for her was to be her best friend. Her mother added that Shea was very nervous about her appearance on the *Today* show, but when she learned that Mercer could accompany her right onto the set, she relaxed and became confident and enthusiastic about it.

Here was a partner and her highly trained assistance dog, dearly loved not for his usefulness as a tool to make life more convenient for a handicapped young lady, but for the deep relationship they share and which has changed her life for the better.

What does this compelling dog and owner relationship look like? How do we know when we have it? What are the slender but powerful threads that span the distance between species and knit us together so tightly with our companion dogs? The assistance and therapy dog trainers have shared many pieces of the puzzle with us about the nature of this deep relationship. Let's try to put them together.

CANINE EMOTIONS: WHERE IT ALL BEGINS

When assistance and therapy dog trainers talk about raising and training the dogs, they use phrases like "building confidence," "decreasing stress," "understanding the dog's physical and mental needs," "supporting the dog," "creating positive experiences for the dog," understanding the dog's "individual personality," and acknowledging the dog's "feelings." Kali Kosch spoke to me about how "quirky" even the most well-trained dog can be and about the need to "spend quality time" with dogs. Nancy Patriarco explained how important touch is to dogs, and Lydia Wade-Driver makes sure her puppy raisers know how to "give and receive love properly" with the dog.

This type of vocabulary, when used to describe something about companion dogs, or about animals in general, was sternly rejected by the scientific community until recently. Researchers considered animals to be robotic creatures that simply reacted to external stimuli with instinctive responses that had nothing to do with feelings and emotions, or even conscious thought. Textbooks contained phrases like "the dog greeted me *as if* it was happy." No credence was given to the idea that the dog might actually *be* happy. Being happy suggests that the animal has emotions, not just instincts.

In his book *The Emotional Lives of Animals,* noted ethologist Marc Bekoff writes about the recent change in this paradigm about animals. He remembers when the scientific community was filled with skeptics about animals having emotions, but now he says, "While debates over *whether* animals have emotions still occur, the question of real importance is becoming *why* animal emotions have evolved the way they have." He adds, "My colleagues and I no longer have to put tentative quotes around such words as *happy* or *sad* when we write about an animal's inner life." In other words, we have begun to recognize that dogs are not "happy," they are happy. We now think of dogs as having real emotions and engaging in conscious thought.

It makes sense that dogs think and have emotions. After all, they share the same biological and chemical systems and structures as humans. Those of us who believe in the theory of evolution would have difficulty making the case for the sudden appearance of emotions in humans while we carefully trace the origin of our other assets from our animal predecessors. Charles Darwin's theory of evolutionary continuity suggests just that: A path of continuity can be established for all aspects of our heritage, not just for some aspects of our heritage. To say that we have many physical characteristics in common with our animal ancestors (including our brains) and then deny the similarity of psychological characteristics makes no sense.

Most scientists agree that emotions are a key to survival for animals. Emotions allow wolves and dogs to live successfully in packs consisting of complex social networks. The members' knowledge of right and wrong behavior, their willingness to care about the welfare of other members as well as their own, and their desire to engage in self-moderated play that instructs but does not harm another pack member all contribute to a thriving group.

Exactly what are these emotions that we share with dogs? Bekoff says, "As a scientist, I feel safe saying that emotions are psychological phenomena that help in behavioral management and control; they are phenomena that emote us, that make us move." Emotions are the body's response to external stimuli, such as the feeling of fear and desire to run away when you see a predator approaching, or the feeling of love that overcomes you in the presence of your offspring.

Why does acknowledging the existence of feelings and emotions in dogs matter? Well, because it's difficult to develop a deep relationship with a robot. Robots possess no emotions and are maintained as tools; dogs are treasured as companions.

In some of the older dog training books on my bookshelves, the authors consistently refer to a dog as "it" in the text, as in, "If your dog does not sit when commanded to sit, push down on *its* rump." Once we acknowledge that our dogs do possess feelings and emotions, our entire relationship with them leaps to a new level. Dogs graduate from an *it* to a *he* or *she*.

What is the difference in your relationship with your car and your best friend? I would guess that you and your friend understand how the other feels about things and you both care deeply about one another's feelings. You base your actions on this level of caring. Your car, on the other hand, performs a useful function. You keep it in the garage, fill it with gas, and use it as it meets your needs. You don't think about your car becoming frightened or bored. Your car doesn't work for you even when it's not well. But you care about your friend when she's upset about missing out on a promotion, and your friend will come to your aid even when she's under the weather. Your car is important to your lifestyle. Your best friend is important to your life. With her you have a deep relationship.

We recognize that the emotions we share with our dogs support the depth of our relationship with them, but how do we read our dog's emotions correctly? Attributing the incorrect emotion to a dog can set us off on the wrong track. For instance, you may think your dog is spiting you by soiling the rug in your absence, but she really feels fear because sometimes when you return home you yell at her for reasons she doesn't understand. It doesn't make sense to her. Your course of action to resolve this problem depends on how well you read the situation, and the wrong course of action could make matters worse. If you continue to yell at your "spiteful" dog, her fear will increase (as will her housespoiling) and the relationship will suffer. If you realize that training is the key and you crate the dog during your absence to prevent accidents, you will return home in a good mood, the dog's fears that develop during your absence will subside, and the problem will disappear with the relationship still intact.

The trainers have taught us to read our dogs carefully and to make well-founded inferences about their emotions. By reading the dog's body language and facial expressions, the trainers can surmise the emotions that accompany them. They can predict what a dog is likely to do next, reason about why she has done something already, and decide how best to respond in a way that builds the relationship and supports the dog's well-being.

In her book *For the Love of a Dog,* applied canine behaviorist Patricia McConnell says, "Accurate, objective observation is a skill that requires practice, but it starts with asking your mind to focus on what you see, not on what you think it means. A very small amount of time and energy spent in reminding your brain to make accurate, objective descriptions of your dog can radically improve the relationship between you and your dog." She continues, "It takes concentration and practice to accurately observe an animal's actions, but it's even harder to develop the discipline to objectively describe the behavior, rather than skipping to a belief about what the animal is thinking or feeling when performing it."

The assistance and therapy dog trainers have taught us how to observe our dogs and communicate with them using some of their own body language and non-verbal signals. We can use these skills to develop accurate descriptions about our dog's behaviors and then interpret the behaviors and their underlying emotions properly.

"We all have filters though which we interpret the world; be careful that yours aren't filtering out who your dog really is," cautions McConnell.

When we acknowledge that our dogs really do experience emotions, and we learn and practice how to observe and interpret their feelings correctly and respond to them using their own language and positive training techniques, we have begun to spin the invisible thread that will connect us forever in a deep relationship.

I'LL KNOW IT WHEN I SEE IT

I was chatting with Lydia in her kitchen one morning when she asked me if I would like to see some pictures of her dogs that might be useful in this book. She brought out a pile of photos through which we browsed. Soon I noticed something interesting about the pictures: In almost every one of them, all the dogs were looking at Lydia. When Lydia was taking the picture, the dogs were looking straight at the camera lens. When someone else was the photographer, all the dogs were looking at Lydia, wherever she was. When Lydia was included in the picture, she was looking at the dogs and not at the camera. After seeing this in photo after photo, the message was clear and stunning: Lydia and her dogs keep in touch through simple eye contact.

I brought my discovery to her attention, and Lydia smiled and said, "Well, I guess you're right about that," as if this was the first time she had noticed it.

"But this habit is one of the first things you train for," I noted. "Here is proof of the success of your training."

"I rather think of it as proof of the success of the relationship," she answered. "I train young dogs to accept and value eye contact, but I don't train the dogs to watch me all the time. We watch each other because we are important to each other. We are connected and want to stay in touch."

I've often asked myself, "How can I know when I have attained a deep and positive relationship with my dog?" My best answer always has been, "I'll know it when I see it." But the assistance and therapy dog trainers have given us clues to evaluating the strength of our relationship with our dogs. These clues are based on subtle habits and behaviors that even physically and mentally handicapped partners use with their dogs with great success.

Remember when Marilyn Wilson taught the puppy raiser class but had the older dog Caesar along with her? She instructed the class but always had her eye on Caesar, whom she was training not to creep forward when put on a "down-stay."

When out and about, the trainers always know exactly where a dog is, they keep the dog in a position where they can see one another's faces, and they make quiet, regular eye contact with each other. The trainers do not give a verbal signal to their dogs by saying "look" or "watch me" every time they want the dog to check in, nor do they reward the dog each time they exchange glances. They just do it casually because this is a way they have adopted to stay connected.

They don't stare at each other either. The human and canine eyes are soft and gentle, the glance momentary. It's quick as a blink, delicate, refined, and oh so powerful. By always staying in a position where the dog can occasionally make eye contact, the trainer is saying to the dog, "I'm here if you need me. I'm always available to you, even if I'm preoccupied with something else." And the dog's eyes answer, "I know you're there, and I'm ready to respond if you need me."

I have witnessed many handlers and dogs spend a full hour working in an obedience or agility class and never once make eye contact. I make it a practice to make eye contact with my dogs on the agility start line. It's our momentary connection just before we meet the challenge of the course together as a team.

I noticed that the assistance dogs also made eye contact with their trainers *before* something happened. For instance, when Lydia and I were having lunch at the café, a woman and her child approached our table to ask if they could pet Aria. Aria noted their approach and quickly flicked her eyes at Lydia before the pair arrived. Lydia, *expecting this communication from Aria and therefore being available to accept it,* returned the look with a miniscule smile and a diminutive cock of her head that Aria interpreted to mean the pair were friendly and she had permission to greet them. It happened in an instant, but there was the brief but unmistakable moment when Aria asked, "Am I free to interact?" and Lydia answered, "Yes."

Many dogs react based only on how they feel at the moment, and only check in with their owners after the fact, if at all. Many dogs would have jumped up to greet the mother and daughter without a glance at their owner, and would have connected with their owner only when they pulled the dog back from leaping on the pair. But assistance and therapy dogs subtly and willingly share the decision-making process with their owners, even if it's done with just a glance. It happens in a flash and without fanfare, but its significance is profound.

The Power of Touch

The trainers use touch with the dogs to accomplish several objectives. Assistance and therapy dogs who are sensitive to touch must learn to accept a bump or a jostle without becoming offended or shying away. Well-intentioned visitors might pet the dog in a way she does not enjoy but must tolerate. For instance, many dogs do not delight in pats on the head and would much rather be stroked on their flank. However, most people aim right for the top of the dog's head when deciding to pet a dog.

We can observe our dog as we pet her and as strangers pet her to determine how she likes to be touched. My terriers enjoy scratches on the chest and shoulders, but dislike head pats. Chase dislikes ear rubs, while Dash finds them relaxing. Chase particularly likes scratches on the top of his rump, while this type of touch annoys Dash.

Touch can also be another way to check in with the dog. When I'm seated in my reading chair, my dogs will sit beside the chair and look up at me. If I merely brush the top of their heads with my fingertips, they will turn and lie down. If they hear a noise outside, lift their heads, and let out a low woof, all I have to do is lightly touch their flanks and they will settle down again. Not a word spoken. That momentary touch, barely a physical connection, is another way in which owners and dogs stay connected.

Suzanne Clothier uses the example of two people going to the movies together. Each person is engaged in the film but is always aware of what is going on with their partner seated next to them. I once was sitting next to my husband in the theater and was quite compelled by the fast-moving plot. However, he shifted a few times in his seat, and I instantly knew that he had pain in his back.

"Have faith in your dog," says Clothier. "He can 'watch the movie' and stay connected with you at the same time."

In a deep relationship, owners stay linked to their dogs with eye contact and casual touch that's pleasing to the dog even when they are distracted by other events. They read each other and communicate with each other through eye contact, verbal signals, body language, expressions, and very subtle physical reactions and responses like a touch or a nudge or a tap. Their radar is always engaged. The quiet conversation never ends.

Respecting Resources

In the wild, canids protect scarce and valuable resources such as food and geographical territory. However, as a working assistance or therapy dog, a canine must give humans access to her possessions and personal space without resistance. The partners can't drag an unwilling dog off the bed or chase her around and then pull a coveted toy out of her mouth. Guarding resources against the intrusion of the partner is counterproductive to the role of an assistance dog, but it's also counter-instinctive for a dog not to guard her resources.

The trainers start by training the dogs to accept human access to their possessions, but then they return the favor—and seal the deal—by respecting the dog's possessions and personal space.

The trainers exchange rewards for toys, rather than forcibly take away the dog's toy. They ask the dog for the toy, reward the dog when she relinquishes it quickly, and often return the toy to the dog immediately as a final reward for her good behavior. They drop special, tasty tidbits into the dog's dinner bowl while the dog is eating her meal. The dog learns to happily anticipate a handler approaching her dinner bowl. The trainers place toys and treats into crates before they confine the dog there, making kenneling an acceptable experience. They don't physically push or pull a dog into or out of a crate; they indicate that the dog should enter or exit under her own power.

But extinguishing resource guarding in dogs represents only half of the equation. The trainers show respect for the dog's possessions and personal space to make sure the dog will not feel the need to protect herself against bullying or rudeness. The trainers don't grab at the dogs or their toys, lean over the dogs, drag them around with a leash, or pull them out from under anything. They make eye contact and speak to the dogs before they take action or ask for a behavior.

Assistance dogs move in and out of the trainers' facility all the time. They come in as puppies, go to a puppy raiser, return to the center for skills training, work and perhaps live with several trainers, and get placed with a recipient. In this constantly changing environment, it would be easy to do the expedient thing and physically manipulate the dogs, become inattentive about which toy or bed belongs to whom, and so on. But the trainers know that deep relationships are built on mutual respect for possessions and the need for some personal space.

I once witnessed an agility competitor run up to her dog in his crate, whip open the crate door, physically pull the dog out and snap on his leash, rush him to the start line, run the dog on the course, pull him back to his crate, and shove him inside, without a word or a glance. She then turned and ran up to the scoreboard to wait for the judges to post the results of her run. "Deep" is not a word I would use to describe that relationship, and I admire her dog for allowing himself to be treated so rudely and still perform in the agility ring, although I do believe their agility career will be a short one.

I have vowed never to place my hand on my dogs' crate door without first looking at him and telling him what's about to happen. They don't understand my words, but they do get a feeling about my intentions.

It's critically important for companion dog owners to teach their dogs not to guard resources and equally important to respect their dog's personal space, because many breeds are especially sensitive to such invasions. Many assistance dogs are sporting breeds, who naturally have few personal space issues. I once talked with a dog breeder about how I had learned to become more aware of canine personal space considerations when I switched from Labrador Retrievers to terriers. "Oh, Labradors," she chuckled. "They're like clowns piling out of a car!" The image of a bunch of Labs heaped into a tiny circus car and then happily tumbling over each other to spill out onto the ground is exactly right. Labs don't take incursions into their personal space all that seriously and are generous with their possessions. But some dogs are not so forgiving, and they require more attention on this issue.

The trainers have taught me that in a deep relationship, handlers combine training to extinguish resource guarding with respectful treatment when it comes to canine resources. The trainers remain mindful that they are exercising control over items (such as toys) or conditions (such as freedom or the ability to interact socially) of high value to the dog, and they do so with care and respect.

Side by Side

Lydia could hardly maneuver from her kitchen table to her counter to refill her coffee cup for the scattering of large dogs all around her kitchen floor. The dogs have almost total run of the house, but they always seem to be where she is. When she left the room to retrieve her photos, most of the dogs got up and went along with her.

At St. Francis, puppies in training, older assistance dogs in training, and the trainers' personal pets mingle in the administrative office area, although they have access to much more space in the building. When one of the trainers leaves the area, her dog(s) follows her. In the puppy raiser training classes, pups and handlers who are not performing an exercise at the moment move to the side of the room and sit together for a rest, mostly with the dog leaning against the puppy raiser's leg.

During a break in Jan Stice's pet therapy class, one handler sat down on the floor and her dog draped himself across her legs and contentedly closed his eyes for a moment's rest.

I attended an AKC Border Terrier specialty show (Border Terriers only) a few years ago and talked with two Border owners who were sharing a motel room at the event. One of the owners laughed about how the other owner's dog slept on the bed with her, both of them snoring. She chuckled to me, "One evening [her roommate] got up from the bed and said offhandedly 'come on Baxter' to her dog. She was headed into the bathroom to take a shower, for heaven's sake! She can't even be separated from him long enough to take a shower!"

One thing is obvious about the deep relationship handlers and partners share with their dogs: They genuinely enjoy each other's company.

Sometimes my husband would like to sit in his chair and read a book without Border Terriers clamoring for a place on his lap. He might like to work on the car or the lawn mower without Chase closely supervising the process with his nose less than an inch from the machine. It might be nice to step around my kitchen without fear of tripping over a dog or dig a hole in the garden without Dash dropping her ball into it before I can get the new plant placed. It's impossible to walk to the mailbox without dogs scampering on my heels.

But I take these as signs that my dogs enjoy being around me as much as I enjoy being around them. I take it as a sign that our commitment to each other stems freely from mutual enjoyment rather than from compulsion. Working, playing, resting, travelling, exercising, training—we enjoy doing these things together.

It's not just because I'm a "dog person" and so automatically take pleasure in the company of dogs. I know a lot of dogs whose habits grate on my last nerve and whom I don't eagerly anticipate seeing. I started by choosing a dog who suited my lifestyle. Then my dogs and I invested years adjusting our relationship to the increased satisfaction of both of us, each willing to make an appropriate accommodation for the other.

From specially bred assistance puppies to hearing dogs of mixed breeding rescued from shelters, the dog and partner relationship has depth when each one places high value on just being in the company of the other.

THE PHILOSOPHERS

I once asked a couple of the assistance dog trainers to sum up their training philosophy in a single sentence. Surprisingly, they didn't have a lot of trouble doing so. With all the dog training literature available today, the amount of training advice on the market is voluminous and complex. But with the assistance dog trainers, I found that the recipe never assumes more importance than the cake—the means are never more important than the end. They are familiar with popular, contemporary dog-training methods and have developed effective methods of their own. But they always maintain the vision of the cake, the end result of the training, above all else. They don't get too bogged down in following the recipe line by line.

I know how to teach agility skills to dogs. However, when my dogs and I come to a tough spot in our training, I sometimes find myself repeating the same methods, hoping I will get a better result "this time"—something like adding more eggs to the recipe each time, hoping the cake will turn out better the next time. But the product of this approach is, of course, frustration, not improvement. My agility instructor often asks me, with a glint in her eye, "So how's that method working for you?," attempting to knock me out of a nonproductive training loop and into thinking about approaching the problem from a different direction.

Assistance dog trainers deal with many dogs and partners each year and can't afford to waste time applying training steps that don't work for a particular dog. They have become fleet-footed, multi-directional trainers who spend time only on methods that work for that particular dog, as long as the method supports the relationship while accomplishing the training goal.

So here are my favorite answers to my question about an underlying training philosophy.

From Brian: "Be an owner and a trainer for *your* dog, not for all dogs."

From Lydia: "What you do as an owner or trainer depends entirely on what your dog does first."

From Jan: "I don't train a dog to react to something in a certain way. I train her to handle things and then *recover and refocus* herself in a certain way."

And, in a recent dog training seminar I attended, Suzanne Clothier added her thinking: "Training isn't about 'things my dog knows'; it's about enhancing the quality of my relationship with my dog."

Each trainer stays focused on the big picture of the desired behavior *and* the nature of the relationship, the "cake," while working through the specific training steps in the recipe.

Assistance dog recipients arrive at the training center and are paired with a young dog who has just completed her formal education at the hands of her puppy raisers and trainers. In just two weeks, they will depart as a team, ready to build on the strong foundation put in place at the center. Each recipient has unique needs, and the trainers cannot anticipate all the specific behaviors each assistance dog may be required to deliver for their partner. But they can anticipate that the development of a deep relationship between the partner and the dog will support existing and future training, no matter what it entails.

In two weeks the trainers can't impart the breadth of the universe of various dog training methods to recipients who may have never owned a dog before. But they can teach the recipients how to understand who their particular dog really is, how to equitably define the possibilities of their relationship with their dog, and how to deepen that relationship with their canine partners.

The rest is icing on the cake.

Afterword

The Truth About Unconditional Canine Love

How many times have you heard a person say, "I like dogs so much because they give their owners unconditional love, no matter what"? About a million times? I have. And I always answer, "Not so!"

Do you believe that dogs whose owners swat them for reasons the dogs don't understand, pull them around on a leash, compel them to spend hours in the yard alone, deny them the company of their family when visitors arrive, subject them to teasing or other invasions of their personal space, or frustrate them because they can't understand their owners' signals and can't make their own feelings clear, really love their owners? They may act in a submissive manner in the presence of their owners. But I don't think they love them.

Dogs are the captives of their owners, but they are really shrewd. They know how to survive and improve their circumstances. They can figure out that angering their owner results in physical punishment or banishment or no play time. They quickly determine how to shape their behavior so that their owner doesn't get angry very often. They nap in a far corner of the room so no one will startle them and accuse them of being in the way. They maintain a low profile, keep a wary eye out, and don't engage until they sense good vibrations exuded by their owner. They hide their toys so they won't get into trouble when they protect them. They fawn upon their owner because their owner seems to respond well to that type of behavior. They stay quiet and passive because the food bowl appears and an occasional walk happens without incident that way. But that's not love; it's strategy.

In contrast, I hope you will enjoy the love of a dog that springs from the investments you have made in your relationship with him. I wish you a dog whose greatest pleasure is to be by your side, a dog who trusts that he is and always will be part of the fabric of your life, a dog who feels understood by you, a dog with the confidence to take a chance and try something new because he knows you will be there to support him, a dog who looks you in the eye and smiles.

Dogs do not bestow this type of love on their owners unconditionally, but it's worth the effort to earn it. They give it in daily doses that accumulate into a lifetime of canine love.

The assistance and therapy dog trainers have traced a map that will guide you in your relationship with your dog. You will discover that the treasures of canine companionship are scattered all along your route, not just at the end of it. Enjoy the journey!

Appendix

Meet the Trainers

They are the quiet trainers. They work in their own homes or in assistance dog training centers, turning out reliable, well-mannered canine partners ready to improve the lives of disabled people year after year. Or they prepare groups of pet dog owners to share the healing companionship of their dogs with others who appreciate it. They are the rarely celebrated gold medalists of dog training, who have contributed their insights to this book and have shown us a path to developing a canine companion whom we welcome into all aspects of our lives and whom others welcome into their lives, too.

Working with them qualifies as one of the most enlightening experiences I have had as a dog owner and trainer. Allow me to introduce some of them to you.

LYDIA WADE-DRIVER

If I were a dog, I would thank my lucky stars if I found myself welcomed into the family pack at Lydia's home. I have never met a trainer who cherishes dogs as much as Lydia.

When she was 3 years old, her mother, who is also fond of dogs, bought Lydia her first dog, a Siberian Husky named Little Wolf, from a breeder. Siberian Huskies are a primitive breed who retain many of the characteristics that made them so valuable to the indigenous tribes of the Arctic north. "He taught me about the strength of canine instincts," she recalls, "and how trainers must acknowledge them and not attempt to train dogs only one way in spite of their instincts."

Later, Princess entered her family. A mixed-breed dog, Lydia found Princess as a stray with a burn wound on her side. A neighbor gave her Kersey, also a mix. Lydia continued to provide a home for needy dogs, including her German Shepherd Dog, Smokey. "I was riding through the woods, admiring the scenery along the roads, when a dog walked out of the trees near the car. I could tell he was starving. I stopped the car, opened the door, and he jumped in. I put up posters describing him, but no one ever claimed him. He lived twelve years and we were inseparable. When I trained other dogs to perform tricks or specific behaviors, Smokey would see the dogs getting treats for their work. He watched the training and then started to perform the behaviors on his own in order to receive the same rewards as the others."

Lydia always wanted to pursue a career in dogs. "I wanted to educate people about how to be better stewards of animals," she says. She researched the field of assistance dog training and enrolled in the Assistance Dog Institute in Santa Rosa, California. She brought her first assistance dog candidate home with her from the institute and started her assistance dog training program in a suburb of Washington, D.C. She acquired a succession of dogs from rescue organizations, shelters, and breeders, but ultimately decided to start her own breeding program. She wanted her female dogs to "mother the puppies" to get them launched on the right track from the beginning. She also needed large, strong dogs in her program for balance assistance work.

"When I start working with a dog," she says, "my first job is to find out who that dog is as an individual, not just their gender or their breed. I go with my gut feeling and start working with them, responding to what I can see are their strong points. For instance, I notice if the dog is very visually oriented, food driven, sound sensitive, or if he values praise highly. I begin the training and immediately customize it for that specific dog as we go along."

Lydia pairs about five assistance dogs with partners each year.

"I'm one of the luckiest people in the world," she says. "I wake up each morning and the first thing I see is all of these dogs that I love."

JAN STICE

As a very small child, Jan began drawing animals. She has surrounded herself with them throughout her life. She showed her horses in fun shows, but did not engage in serious competition with her horses or dogs. "I just like having fun with my animals," she says. "I don't care who's the best."

A retired medical secretary living in southwest Virginia, Jan became involved with the Delta Society's Pet Partners Program about six years ago as a way to "help me share my love of animals with other people." As a former healthcare administrator, Jan had interacted with many seniors during her career. "I have always enjoyed older folks," she says with a smile.

Jan engages in pet-assisted therapy activities with her three dogs: Crystal, a 6-year-old Border Collie–Golden Retriever mix whom she rescued from the Roanoke Valley SPCA at 3 months of age; Lucas, a Golden Retriever–Collie mix surrendered to a shelter in North Carolina at 3 years of age when his owners moved out of the country; and Faith, a 5-year-old Border Collie–Golden Retriever mix who had been tied up in a yard without adequate food or water until the neighbors alerted the local authorities.

Five of the teams I observed in her therapy dog training class participated in a reading program for children in the first through sixth grades at a branch of the local library. Teachers sent a few of their students who had reading difficulties to attend the three two-hour sessions where the kids read, one-on-one, to a dog. The children, reluctant readers in the past, spent hours picking out just the right book to read to the dog. Several mothers commented that their children pestered them all week about not forgetting their appointment to read to the dog.

"I was so thrilled watching the teams," Jan says. "These were people I trained and they were sharing their dogs to benefit the lives of others."

"Of course," she adds with a twinkle in her eye, "all of the owners participating are driven by the motivation to help others, but the owners and their dogs come away from the sessions having gained so much for themselves. But that's our little secret."

As pet-assisted therapy earns more attention from the public, Jan responds to requests to make presentations to senior groups, dog training clubs, hospices, veterinary open houses, and health fairs. She works with a hospice organization, taking her dogs to meet with and comfort children who have recently lost a parent. She visits nursing homes, where one of her dog's biggest fans scans the activities calendar to be sure she knows when the dogs will visit and plants herself by the front door because "she always wants to be the first one to see my dogs on visiting day."

In a recent visit to a rehabilitation center, Jan brought her dog to a rehab session for an elderly lady who had not been responding well to the challenges of physical therapy. When the patient caught sight of Jan's dog, she burst into tears and hugged the dog tightly, telling Jan how much she missed her own dog. Jan spied the therapist writing notes in her log book. Always sensitive about not disrupting medical procedures during her visits, Jan was concerned the therapist might indicate that the presence of Jan's dog delayed the progress of the rehab session. She checked with the therapist. "I no longer have any 'progress goals' established for this session," the therapist answered softly. "Your dog is performing all the therapy this patient needs today."

NANCY PATRIARCO

A retired registered nurse, Nancy trained Tyler, an Australian Shepherd and the first assistance dog graduated from St. Francis of Assisi Service Dog Foundation in Roanoke, Virginia, in the mid-1990s. Nancy established and documented the training program that launched St. Francis and continues to advise the center about its training program today.

She brought probationary assistance-dogs-in-training home to live with her to determine their potential as assistance dogs. Whenever a breeder donated an adult dog to the program, Nancy boarded the dog in her home for a month to assess his suitability for a career as an assistance dog. Today, Nancy serves as an advisor to the training staff and puppy raisers at St. Francis.

Nancy's Labrador Retriever, Lyra, worked as an ambassador dog for St. Francis. Nancy socialized and trained Lyra in all the assistance dog behaviors and Lyra demonstrated the behaviors at special events. "The center needed a demo dog," says Nancy, "but the dogs-in-training didn't know all of the behaviors yet and it's not always good to take them out and ask them to perform in pubic before they have established good self-confidence. So Lyra helped us."

Nancy showed her Shetland Sheepdog and her German Shepherd Dog in AKC obedience competition. Currently, she lives with two Border Collies, Kismet, who is 8 years old, and Anna, who is 2 years old. Kismet has earned his AKC Obedience Trial Champion (OTCh) title, a much-coveted indication of the close working relationship between a highly competitive obedience dog and his skillful handler. Nancy is working with Anna in herding events and competitions.

Nancy follows a balanced approach to dog training. "Of course, I never use hurtful methods," she explains. "But I provide positive reinforcements along with negative indicators when a dog makes a mistake. Mostly, a verbal 'uh-oh' is all that's needed to indicate a negative reaction to a dog's behavior. The dog deserves to receive clear information about his behavioral choices. Exclusively negative training creates fear behaviors and bad attitudes in dogs. Exclusively positive training, with no negative indicators at all, causes dogs to become insecure. Dogs naturally establish and honor limits within their packs. In the wild, they acknowledge and observe social and behavioral boundaries very well. As our pets, they seek to find information about these same limits from their leaders—their owners."

KALI KOSCH

As a child, Kali trained her first dog, a Lab named Brandy, at a local 4H club. Her parents home-schooled Kali and required that she participate in some type of community service activity as part of her educational experience. At 15 years old, she chose to volunteer at Assistance Dogs of America (ADA) in Swanton, Ohio.

During her first year, she spent most of her time grooming and exercising the dogs and doing some basic training. Later, the center offered her a part-time job as a training apprentice, where she received lots of on-the-job training, along with attending seminars, conferences, and reading books about training dogs. She worked with Brandy at home and taught her all the assistance dog behaviors.

Kali became a full-time trainer for ADA and eventually was promoted to director of training. The center graduates about twenty teams a year.

In addition to matching assistance dogs with disabled partners, Kali places full-time, on-site therapy dogs. If a dog drops out of the assistance dog program due to a mild physical problem or a behavioral quirk, but would otherwise make a wonderful companion, Kali matches them with an opportunity to be an on-site therapy dog. "Sometimes children with autism or other disabilities don't need a dog to perform complex helping behaviors for them. They simply benefit from the constant companionship of a well-trained dog in their home. We place some therapy dogs in schools, where they live with the student counselor who brings the dog to school each day. The teachers use time with the dog as a reward for the students and arrange for some children to read to the dog. We can also make placements in hospices and nursing homes, where the dog lives in the facility full-time. We train the dog and then train the dog's caretaker about how to manage the dog on site."

Kali shares her home with a Boxer-Shepherd mix whom she plans to train in search-and-rescue work.

MARILYN WILSON

Fifteen years ago, Marilyn jumped with both feet into the world of dogs when she got her first Newfoundland. Today, she has two Newfs, Scout and Jefferson, and has participated in obedience training and competition, tracking, agility, *draught work* (weight pulling), and water rescue exercises with her dogs.

She loved training her dogs and wanted to "take my knowledge and put it to use to benefit other people who owned or worked with dogs." Four years ago, Marilyn began to volunteer at St. Francis of Assisi Service Dog Foundation. When a position opened up as a staff trainer and program manager of the puppy raiser division, Marilyn applied for and got the assignment.

At any one time, Marilyn manages about twelve puppies placed in private puppy raiser homes or at a local prison as part of the center's Prison Pup program.

Carefully selected prisoners help raise future assistance dogs by teaching behaviors and caring for the young dogs. The dogs spend some of their time with families to receive the proper amount of socialization along with their behavior training.

Marilyn and her husband, Art, teach tracking classes for a local dog training club. Previously, she taught obedience and canine behavior modification privately, but the requirements of her work at St. Francis leave her little time to do so now.

The newest addition to her canine family has just arrived: a Gordon Setter puppy, Mia. After carefully researching a breed that would complement her existing pack and lifestyle, Marilyn welcomed Mia into the group and plans to show her in conformation events and handle her in sporting dog field trials, along with obedience, tracking, and agility. Marilyn plans to teach Mia all the assistance dog behaviors so she can become an ambassador dog for St. Francis.

She brings Mia to work with her at the center, where dogs interact freely all day and visitors come and go, so you know the pup's black-belt socialization training will begin immediately.

"I start by developing a relationship with a dog," says Marilyn, "and then I use training to strengthen it. For my dogs, training is the same as play and games; it's an enjoyable, everyday event."

KAREN HOUGH

At the age of 7, Karen noticed a Border Collie–type of mixed-breed dog eating from the Dumpster behind a grocery store near her New Mexico home. The dog appeared every time her family shopped. One day, the dog was standing on top of a pile of onions that the store had discarded. Karen brought the stray dog home and named him Onion.

While living in Houston, Karen acquired her next dog, a Border Collie named Radar. She enrolled in a basic dog obedience class and "had so much fun that we just kept on going." She showed Radar in AKC obedience trials and taught him agility skills.

When she moved to Roanoke, Virginia, Karen and Radar became one of three founding owner-handler teams of a new dog training club. With membership numbering about one hundred today, the club offers classes in obedience, agility, tracking, therapy dog training, rally obedience, conformation handling, trick training, and more to hundreds of students each year.

Karen is a former training director for St. Francis of Assisi Service Dog Foundation and adopted one of the center's "career change" dogs, a Border Collie named Stony. A *career change dog* is one who has begun training for assistance dog work but has developed a minor physical problem or a behavioral habit that is inappropriate for assistance dogs. The trainers arrange for the dog to become a pet in someone's home.

Later, a breeder of Australian Shepherds contacted St. Francis and offered to donate an adult dog to the program. At the time, the center had reached its capacity for adult dogs, but Karen decided that there was a place for the dog in her family and she adopted Megan, a one-and-a-half year old Aussie. Megan and Karen became a Delta Society certified pet-partner team and worked together in agility.

Always a fan of herding dogs, Karen added Tango, a male Smooth Collie, to her family and works with him in AKC rally and obedience competition.

In 2005, Karen left her position at St. Francis to launch her Field of Dreams Dog Training business. She teaches group classes in agility, puppy life skills for dogs less than 5 months old, and pet manners for adult dogs. She also teaches individual dog and owner teams privately, including preparing dogs to become assistance dogs. She has added two part-time trainers to her fast-growing business and a local doggie daycare center has asked her to teach evening classes for their clients at their facility.

Karen is a Certified Pet Dog Trainer (CPDT), having joined the Association of Pet Dog Trainers and completed their program of study and testing.

In addition to managing her business, Karen works with the local SPCA to socialize and train dogs at the shelter to make them more adoptable.

"I borrowed my first rule of dog training from the medical community," Karen says. "'Do no harm' is my guiding principle when training dogs and their owners. I don't allow the use of abusive techniques or equipment; I don't use prong collars, choke chains, or electronic collars in my business. I can achieve excellent results without them. I concentrate on motivating the owners with positive feedback, just like I motivate the dogs. I want the owners to know the 'why' about dog training, not just the 'how.'"

CONNIE KNISELY

"As a kid, I watched assistance dogs and decided I wanted to train them," says Connie. Ten years ago she joined St. Francis of Assisi Service Dog Foundation as a field trainer.

She has welcomed a number of dogs into her family over the years, including a Schnauzer mix named Camper, a stray whom park rangers found wandering in a campground, a Labrador Retriever mix, a Catahoola Leopard Dog, a Beagle, and a Shetland Sheepdog mix.

She trained a dog in narcotics detection work and tracking, and sold the dog to the West Virginia State Police. Connie worked for a private company training explosive detection dogs for the United States government. Along with a Belgian Malinois and an Akita-Lab mix, she trained several Australian Shepherds in this task and they eventually became known as the Aussie Posse because of their successful field work.

Today, Connie shares her home with two Chinese Cresteds and a black Lab. She trained 12-year-old Nik, her Lab, as a narcotics detection dog and he has earned several AKC obedience titles. Tsunami, her 4-year-old Chinese Crested, competes in agility and obedience trials. Both Tsunami and Mister Spock, her 14-year-old Chinese Crested, are certified Delta Society Pet Partners.

Connie works with adult St. Francis dogs at the conclusion of their training, when they are polishing their behavior skills, and she arranges for their placement with a partner. Connie teaches foster family classes for families who volunteer to provide homes for the assistance dogs-in-training.

Connie advises owners and trainers to adapt to their dog's individual characteristics and to the specific situation in which the dog must live and work. "There are no cookie cutters in my training tool box," she says. "You might think that dogs are all the same, but they're definitely not."

About the Author

Lorie Long has been raising and training dogs for more than twenty-five years. While living in a suburb of Washington, D.C., Lorie served in several officer positions, including president, for the Dulles Gateway Obedience Training Club. She taught classes in beginner and intermediate dog obedience at the club, and competed in American Kennel Club obedience trials. She also worked her dogs in tracking.

In addition, she provided customized, individual dog training and canine behavior modification services through her private canine consulting business.

Lorie participated in therapy dog visits at a northern Virginia nursing home with her Labrador Retrievers and wrote about a New Jersey nursing home's resident therapy dog for *DogWorld* magazine.

Currently, Lorie is a member and instructor at the Star City Canine Training Club in Roanoke, Virginia. She teaches basic dog obedience training skills to novice dog owners and introductory agility training skills to handlers who are new to the sport.

An active agility competitor, Lorie trains and competes with her two Border Terriers, Dash and Chase. Both dogs have multiple advanced agility titles and Dash has earned the coveted AKC title, Master Agility Champion.

Lorie regularly attends seminars and workshops addressing a wide variety of topics, including dog training methods, holistic veterinary care, canine relationship building, and structural care for the canine athlete.

A member of the Dog Writers Association of America, Lorie has written about dogs for the *Whole Dog Journal*, *DogWorld*, and *Chesapeake Bay* magazine. She is the author of *The Siberian Husky*.

Her research for the article "We Can Help" (*Whole Dog Journal*, April 2005), which highlighted the socialization methods used by assistance dog trainers, was the inspiration for *A Dog Who's Always Welcome*.

Lorie would enjoy hearing from readers. You can reach her at lorielong1@ gmail.com.

Index

CPSIA information can be obtained
at www.ICGtesting.com
Printed in the USA
BVHW02s0244091117
499880BV00009B/212/P